# DIANA
## Princess of Wales

# THE
# BOOK
# OF
# FASHION

First published in Great Britain by Colour Library Books Ltd.
© 1983 Illustrations and text: Colour Library Books Ltd.,
   Guildford, Surrey, England.
Display and text filmsetting by Acesetters Ltd., Richmond, Surrey, England.
Printed and bound in Barcelona, Spain by JISA-RIEUSSET and EUROBINDER.
ISBN 0 86283 120 2

DLB 37981-83

£4.50

# DIANA
## Princess of Wales

# THE
# BOOK
# OF
# FASHION

TEXT BY

## Jane Owen

**Produced by**
**TED SMART AND DAVID GIBBON**

## COLOUR LIBRARY BOOKS

Waving two Union Jacks as if their lives depended on it and screaming "Over here Princess Diana, *pleeeeeease*", two little boys managed at last to attract the attention of Diana, Princess of Wales. She crossed her walkabout route to talk to them and, holding a man's black umbrella against the pouring rain, she asked with a large, encouraging smile, "You look very wet – have you been waiting long?" They nodded, squirmed with delighted embarrassment at meeting the beautiful Princess, and then pushed a bunch of drooping wild flowers into her hand. "Ah, are these for me...lovely...thank you, now you can go home and dry off", she said. The boys were struck dumb by their Royal encounter and turned to bury their faces in their mother's skirt. Their mother was beaming from ear to ear. "I just never believed she would see them. Isn't she beautiful...so kind...her eyes are so beautiful", she murmured. The Princess had made another conquest, this time on a walkabout at Pupuke boating centre in New Zealand. It had looked so easy – the few well-chosen words, the sweet smile and the charming manner. The Princess has the style to carry out her work as if it were second nature, and at just 22 years of age she makes her meetings with statesmen look as easy as that with the little boys. Perhaps her easy-going nature is one of the qualities which attracted Prince Charles. By the time he met Lady Diana he had known more than his fair share of beautiful, clever and talented women but she had that extra special something. There is no doubt Lady Diana was born with that elusive quality, 'style'. Her clothes show it – her dress sense has rekindled the British rag trade – and so does her ability to cope with the Royal job. In the face of relentless public scrutiny the Princess has remained charming, uncomplaining and good-natured, and, in good times and bad alike, she has always maintained her dignity. This is the story of the Princess' style and how it developed as she became a leading Royal lady. It is a story that is linked, inevitably, with her love affair with the Prince, and the events leading up to their romance and marriage.

Prince Charles first set eyes on his future Princess one winter afternoon at a Park House tea party. Park House was the Spencer home, just a quarter of a mile from Sandringham, the Royal Family's Norfolk retreat until 1975. It was around Christmas time and sixteen-year-old Prince Charles popped his head round the nursery door on his way back from an outing with the grown-ups. His brother, Prince Andrew, was having tea with one or two local children...including three-year-old, blonde-haired, blue-eyed Diana Spencer, who wore a smocking dress for the occasion. Neither the Prince nor the Princess remember that first meeting so many years ago – it was the nanny in charge of Diana at the time, Miss Janet Thompson, who recalls it so vividly. It is well recorded that the first time they remember meeting each other was some years later when Prince Charles stayed at Althorp, the Spencer family home, for a shoot. "I remember thinking what a jolly and amusing and attractive sixteen year old she was. I mean, great fun, bouncy and full of life and everything", said Prince Charles when he looked back on that day at Althorp. She saw things in a rather more positive light and said she found Prince Charles "pretty amazing". Was it then the fresh-faced teenager set her heart on becoming the Princess of Wales? If her school pin-up was anything to go by it was – for while the other girls fixed pop idols and film stars to the walls, Lady Diana pinned up a picture of Prince Charles. Three years later the courtship began in earnest with a few Royal dates during the summer of 1980, including one to watch the Prince playing polo, another to spend some time on board *Britannia* during Cowes Week and, finally, an invitation to the Royal Family's Highland home, Balmoral. It was there in the balmy Balmoral autumn that the young couple began to recognise their love for each other, although the romance may have been a little one sided to begin with. But Lady Diana *knew* she was right for the Prince – and perhaps it was her single-minded determination, her unflagging love and loyalty which won the Prince's heart as much as her prettiness and charm.

The Princess of Wales is one of a dying race – an old-fashioned girl. But, as became apparent in the winter of 1980-1981, she was also canny enough to know how to manage the Press. The Press thundered into Lady Diana's quiet life that autumn when she was staying at Balmoral as the guest of the Queen. She was also there to help look after her sister's first baby – her sister, Lady Jane, is married to Robert Fellowes, Assistant Private Secretary to the Queen. During Lady Diana's stay there it was clear that the bond between her and Prince Charles was strengthening. When the Press got wind of a possible romance, the tranquillity of the Highland holiday was shattered by car chases, long-distance photographs of Lady Diana out fishing with the Prince and endless 'phone calls to anyone who might be able to throw light on the young couple's relationship. On her return to London Lady Diana's flat came under siege, and sometimes her daily routine would be monitored by eager reporters and photographers. But Lady Diana kept her head and concocted a new and highly successful formula for dealing with the Press. Unlike her sister, Lady Sarah, who had been on first name terms with many of those on her heels during her close friendship with Prince Charles, Lady Diana was on surname terms only. She was friendly but formal – polite but never chummy. Her plan worked well, and so impressed many of the pressmen who had closely watched Prince Charles' girlfriends over the years that she could count a handful of journalists as well as a Prince among her admirers. Not bad for a 19 year old.

Lady Diana's mature, dignified personality had made itself obvious from an early age when she was nicknamed 'Duchess' by the family. Those who remember her as a little girl growing up at Park House and later at Althorp say she was kind, thoughtful and altogether a 'nice girl' as the Princess' hatter John Boyd would say about her even today. Little Diana had two nannies – Judith Parnell of Kent and Janet Thompson of Cambridge, and a governess, Miss Gertrude Allen or 'Ally' who looked after Diana's mother when she was a girl. Ally, who died in 1981, used to recall that her charge never liked her lessons as much as outdoor games – especially swimming. But all the same Diana tried hard at her writing and reading lessons, and according to Miss Allen she was "a conscientious girl. Not particularly bright...But she loved stories about kings and queens, especially stories with happy endings." Her father remembers her at this time being a "very sweet-natured girl. She loved her soft toys almost as much as she loved babies. She always loved babies." Sweet-natured girl though she was, she also had a strong personality.

Janet Thompson remembers how Diana had to be scolded when she started to pull off the crusts from her nursery tea sandwiches and leave them to one side, instead of eating them as she had been told. Duly, and to Miss Thompson's satisfaction the crusts disappeared. It was some weeks later that Miss Thompson discovered a little pile of crusts secreted on a hidden ledge under the nursery table. These were the days when her brother Charles, three years her junior, was still a baby and Diana used to mother him and care for him almost as if she were his mother. But, Nanny Thompson says, Diana's sweet nature did not make her a pushover. According to Miss Thompson, the other side of Diana's personality was "very strong-willed".

A weaker will than Lady Diana's would probably have been broken under the strain of constant public attention and Press comment. In those early years Diana was being brought up like any young lady of her class. Already, some say with hindsight, there were all the signs that Diana was destined for greater things. Diana earned her nickname 'Duchess' because she was self-possessed and carried herself with near-regal grace from an early age. But she was never aloof and Alfred Betts, one of the Spencers' butlers, tells how Diana used to do all her own domestic chores, iron her jeans and pack her trunk and tuck box for school. School does not seem to have made much impact on Diana. First she went to Silfield in King's Lynn and then to Riddlesworth Hall preparatory school where she boarded for two years – by the time she arrived there she was nine. Staff there remember her joining in all the usual St Trinian-style pranks such as making apple-pie beds. But the headmistress Miss Ridsdale, now retired, confesses "I can't remember her awfully well...What stands out in my mind is how awfully sweet she was with the little ones." It has been well recorded that Diana was not over-fond of academic life but that is part of the Spencer tradition. Diana's grandfather the 7th Earl Spencer once confessed in a speech to Northampton County School, "When I was a boy at school I would have been glad to have hanged the writer of the Latin grammar, to have drawn the author of the arithmetic book and to have quartered the man who tabulated French irregular verbs...I should also liked to have hanged, drawn and quartered the writer of the Greek grammar."

At Lady Diana's next school, West Heath School near Sevenoaks, history repeated itself – Lady Diana did well at sports and less well at her books. She continued to work hard at her dancing lessons, but her ambition to be a ballet dancer was clearly impossible because she was growing too tall. The headmistress, Miss Ruth Rudge, remembers, "She's a girl who notices what needs to be done and then does it willingly and cheerfully". When she was 14, the seventh Earl Spencer died and Diana's family moved from Park House at Sandringham to the family stately home Althorp, and it was there on one of Althorp estate's ploughed fields that the Prince of Wales and his bride first remember meeting each other. She was introduced to Charles by her sister Lady Sarah, a close friend of the Prince. It was a friendship which taught Lady Diana a great deal.

Lady Sarah had been seen so often with the Prince, and the couple were obviously so fond of each other that many assumed they would marry. Lady Sarah, as she revealed later, had only ever been a friend to the Prince, and found their well-publicised relationship something of a burden because she was going out with another man at the time. Things came to a head when Lady Sarah was asked by a woman's magazine for an interview on the slimmers' disease anorexia nervosa, from which Lady Sarah had suffered. During the interview Lady Sarah explained that she and Prince Charles were genuinely 'just good friends' and that she could never marry him. True though her revelations were, they were badly received at Buckingham Palace – and her close friendship with the Prince came to an abrupt end. To adolescent Lady Diana the episode was a lesson she took to heart, and partly explains why she treated the Press with such maturity when her turn came to be followed by them.

Like Lady Sarah, Lady Diana decided to go to a Swiss finishing school, Institut Alpin Videmanette near Gstaad, where well-brought up young ladies were expected to brush up their French, cooking, typing and dressmaking. It was there she discussed her future plans with her French teacher who later recalled, "Lady Diana was broad-minded but she was also very idealistic about what she wanted for herself. She knew she wanted to work with children – and then she wanted to get married and have children of her own." But Diana, who left West Heath aged 16 – against her father's advice – stayed only one term at finishing school and returned to London in March 1978. There and in Hampshire she played nanny to one or two families, then she did a Cordon Bleu cookery course in Wimbledon and lived in her mother's Cadogan Square flat. After a spell at Madame Vacarni's dancing school trying unsuccessfully to learn to be a ballet teacher, her parents bought Lady Diana a flat in Coleherne Court, Chelsea, for about £50,000, and it was there she began life as an independent bachelor girl, sharing the flat with three girlfriends.

A few months later she landed a job as a teacher at the New England Kindergarten in Pimlico. Lady Diana, "A pied piper with children" according to her mother, was in her element, and three afternoons a week she would jump on her bike or behind the wheel of her VW (after she crashed the VW her father gave her a Metro) and go to the little school to paint, dance, and build models with her toddler charges – they adored her as much as she loved them. On the other two afternoons she used to look after a little American boy. For someone with Lady Diana's love of children it was a charmed existence. At her Coleherne Court home, too, she seems to have been very happy. Her flatmates, Carolyn Pride, Virginia Pitman and Anne Bolton were loyal and friendly company – even if they were a little untidy by Lady Diana's standards. She would regularly tidy up and keep the place clean for them all – her natural home loving, domesticated personality was becoming ever more obvious. Unlike many girls of her age she was not boy mad – she certainly had more than her fair share of suitors but, or so it appeared to those who knew her, she never seemed interested in even the most eligible young men in pursuit...it was if she was in love with someone else. Lady Diana seems to have been a dreamy young lady in many respects – her flatmates once or twice returned to find her dancing, quite alone, around the drawing room in the flat to some of her favourite pop songs.

Like any girl of her class Lady Diana spent many weekends away in the country – then there were all the usual dances and parties to which she was invited. But during the week she liked nothing better than strolling around some of London's grandest shops. Harvey Nichols and Harrods were favourites, and apart from buying the odd piece of kitchen equipment or knickknack for the flat Lady Diana spent many an hour browsing through the dress racks in those shops. Later, after her engagement, it was at Harvey Nichols, in a special private room, that Lady Diana used to entertain some of her friends to lunch. But in her pre-engagement days when plain Lady Diana could expect no such special treatment she used sometimes to take tea with a friend in Fortnum and Mason where she could also buy some of her best-loved goodies. She has a very sweet tooth and, before she was married, she enjoyed eating sweets, such as Yorkie bars, toffees, Roses chocolates, fudge and Revels and others. Sometimes Lady Diana would make her way up to the other end of London to see the latest creations in Bond Street or to look at fabrics in Liberty's – and, of course, there were frequent calls on her sister, Lady Jane Fellowes, who lives in Kensington Palace.

In the summer of 1979 Lady Diana was invited by the Queen to Balmoral – the idea was that she and Prince Andrew might hit it off. There is no doubt they were and still are good friends – but there was no question of romance. However, the young Prince did point out to his big brother Prince Charles that Lady Diana was a good-looking girl and a real charmer. Still nothing happened when Lady Diana went to Sandringham in February 1980 – but then there were several invitations from the Prince of Wales himself. The first clue to the outside world that Lady Diana was a new contender for Prince Charles' heart was at Cowes Week, when Prince Philip invited her aboard *Britannia*. The carefree Lady Diana was responsible for one of the heir to the throne's tumbles into the sea from his windsurfer when she playfully pulled at the mast and upset his balance. A few watching from nearby Press boats assumed this must be Lady Sarah, who had put back a little of the massive amount of weight she lost while suffering from the slimmers' disease anorexia nervosa, and was looking much better for it – few guessed then who this young lady really was, and those who did never guessed the significance of her presence.

To Lady Diana's flatmates it was obvious that romance was in the air – she was even more dreamy than usual, happier and preoccupied. And she seemed to be going on an extraordinary number of clandestine dates. Lady Diana would only admit she had fallen in love with someone called Charles Renfrew (one of the Prince's eleven titles is Baron Renfrew). Already she was beginning to get the hang of being girlfriend to the heir to the throne. She would ring Charles' valet Stephen Barry, say where she would be at what time – usually at her grandmother's house in Eaton Square or her sister's Kensington Palace home – and Stephen would pick her up to take her to wherever the Prince happened to be. But by this time, despite elaborate undercover getaway plans, the Press always found out if the Prince and Lady Diana had turned up at one of the Royal homes such as Sandringham. The siege tactics became too much for the young couple and indeed for the rest of the Royal Family – and so the Prince decided that in future the odd days off in the country would have to be snatched at the only half-finished Highgrove, his newly acquired Cotswold home.

That Christmas Prince Charles, cautious to the last, discussed the possibility of marriage with Lady Diana. The proposal for which Lady Diana longed came at an intimate Buckingham Palace dinner in Prince Charles' apartments on February 5th, 1981. Lady Diana was on the point of leaving for Australia to stay with her mother, Mrs Shand Kydd, and her stepfather on their New South Wales' property. The Prince proposed and although he admitted he had not gone down on both or even one knee, and Lady Diana accepted without hesitation, he told her to think about it – but she was sure and as she later said, "It wasn't a difficult decision in the end – it was what I wanted, it is what I want...I never had any doubts about it." Lady Diana's unwavering conviction that she and the Prince were made for each other had won through.

Brimming with happiness over her still-secret engagement to her Prince, Lady Diana flew back to England a week early. That Sunday, February 22nd, Lady Diana dined with the Queen at Windsor Castle, and after dinner looked through a tray of rings from the Royal jewellers Garrards and chose a large sapphire and diamond ring. Meanwhile the Prince had rung Earl Spencer to ask for his daughter's hand in marriage. Bubbling with excitement, but still unable to break the secret, Lady Diana went to work at the kindergarten on Monday, February 23rd, as usual, and in the evening went to the Palace where she and Prince Charles were joined for drinks by Earl Spencer and Lady Diana's stepmother Raine, whose mother Barbara Cartland writes romantic novels with story lines about pure and lovely young ladies marrying handsome princes.

At 10.40 on February 24th the Prince arrived at a meeting of his household and introduced them to the future Princess of Wales. Twenty minutes later the news was made official by Buckingham Palace, and at the same moment policemen arrived to guard Lady Diana's Coleherne Court flat. Her life as an aristocratic member of the public was over. Outside the Palace Earl Spencer was posing for photographers holding his own camera in one hand. He has always taken photographs of his daughter on important occasions during her life – this was no exception. He explained that the photographs would be added to his rather modestly named 'scrapbooks'. In fact they are large, leather-bound books which contain letters to, and sometimes from, each of his children plus photographs of them from the year dot. Eighteen months later Earl Spencer was once more one of the first photographers on the spot when the Princess had her first baby. Inside the palace, as the flowers and telegrams started to pour in, everyone, from the most prominent page to the youngest housemaid, was given a glass of champagne.

With two detectives now assigned to her, the almost daily flattering features in newspapers about her, and with the universal public approval of her, Lady Diana's new position might have gone to her head. But it didn't. She was obviously determined to show that she wouldn't be spoiled by all the attention. She remained polite and self-effacing to everyone. Even the palace servants found her well mannered and undemanding when she lived there – in the suite consisting of a sitting room, bathroom and bedroom once used by Miss Peebles, the Royal governess. If Lady Diana wanted a snack she would trot down the long corridors to the other end of the palace to get herself something to eat rather than trouble the footman assigned to her. But, despite her informal attitude, which charmed the palace staff, no one was left in any doubt as to who was in charge. As with her successful dealings with the Press, Lady Diana kept her relationship with the people who looked after her on a friendly but formal basis. Once more the formula worked.

On top of having to learn to *be* Royal, Lady Diana was making her first moves to dress like a Royal Lady. Her 'Sloane Ranger' style had been just the thing for an aristocratic girl about town. Her cotton print skirts, quilted jackets, strings of pearls and neckerchiefs was, and is, the only uniform for any well-brought-up 'Sloane' – and off duty it is a style the Princess still favours. But it is not suitable for an on-duty future Queen. Luckily, Lady Diana's mother, the Hon Mrs Shand Kydd – divorced from Earl Spencer in April 1969 – and her sisters, Lady Jane and Lady Sarah, are all fashion buffs and could guide Diana through the fashion maze. The first problem for Lady Diana to tackle was what to wear on the day her engagement was announced. She had already agreed to an interview in the morning, followed by a photo call for the world's Press in the afternoon. Her clothes would have to be pretty but sensible, grand enough for a future king's fiancée, and simple enough to look elegant in the black and white, and colour, photographs that would be published worldwide.

The Princess-to-be began her clothes hunt at Simpson's in Piccadilly, but the shop couldn't offer her what she was looking for. She found what she wanted in Harrods, three days before the official announcement of the engagement – an off-the-peg, blue silk suit with a blue and white blouse, by Cojana. On the day the engagement was announced Lady Diana wore a red velvet suit, with red shoes and stockings, for a Press interview. For the picture session that followed she changed into the blue Cojana suit, the skirt of which had been lengthened in case anyone thought it too daring. There was no danger of that – the suit looked pretty enough, but it was a little too respectable, even middle-aged, for the slim, pretty Diana. Once again, Mrs Shand Kydd stepped in and, this time, just a few days after the engagement, she took Lady Diana to see some of London's top designers: Jean Muir, Belinda Bellville and David Sassoon, Bill Pashley and the all-important hatter John Boyd.

John Boyd, a charming, soft-spoken Scotsman, is the Princess' only hat designer, although she buys standard headgear, such as hard hats for riding, from Lock's in St James's. In the early engagement days Lady Diana would rush into John Boyd's tiny, Brompton Arcade hatshop (he is about to move to Walton Street) to ask for hats – usually at very short notice – to go with her latest dress buys. It was hard for him to explain to the enthusiastic young lady that he needed more than just a belt or a scrap of material from an outfit to know what kind of hat to make for her. "But she is such a *nice* wee girl. So polite..." says John. Today he sometimes takes his creations to the Princess – but frequently he has to ring dress designers to find out exactly the kind of outfit he has to make a hat to go with. Lady Diana was new to the hat world, so John Boyd would show her how each new pillbox, boater, veiled or brimmed hat should be worn. Not that she always followed his advice; even today she prefers to wear some of them sideways – or back to front!

Bellville Sassoon, the Belinda Bellville and David Sassoon partnership of over twenty years standing, was one of the Princess-to-be's first favoured designers. Princess Alexandra and the Duchess of Kent are regular customers so they are used to dressing fashion conscious Royal Ladies. One of their first designs for Diana was the navy blue and white sailor suit she wore for the pictures taken with the Queen and Prince Charles to celebrate the Privy Council's approval of the marriage, and later the coral-pink silk dress and jacket going away outfit. With alternative long-sleeved or short-sleeved jackets to go with the dress, it is an outfit the Princess regularly wears for official engagements. But their most enduring success to date is the filmy, hand-painted chiffon crinoline, off-the-shoulder dress in pinks and blues which the Princess has worn several times. The dress looked its best at the premiere of *Gandhi* where it was set off against the Princess' bouquet of mauvey-pink orchids. Just after her engagement Diana and her mother swooped into Bellville Sassoon's Pavilion Road salon with very little ceremony. Even now the Princess sometimes arrives at her favourite haute couture designers without much warning, to browse through their rails and have a chat about their latest designs, on one of her London shopping sprees.

Bellville Sassoon's clothes – beautifully cut and styled – can, nevertheless, be worn only by those with a figure as good as the Princess. The dramatic features which are so much a part of the clothes – sailor suits, broad sailor collars with frilly edges, and seven-eighths coats – would probably look ridiculous on anyone shorter or plumper than the Princess. But, as any designer will agree, her 22-inch waist and 5ft 10-inch frame provide ideal statistics for the wearing of elegant fashions.

Another already-Royal designer who won Lady Diana's admiration was Caroline Charles. She designs for the Duchess of Kent and for Princess Margaret at her Beauchamp Place salon, and during the Sixties she was apprenticed to Mary Quant. In September 1981 the Princess wore a Caroline Charles red and black plaid suit to the Braemar Games, and early in 1983 a cool grey silk jacket and skirt to an on-tour engagement in Australia. But Diana was already an old fan of Caroline Charles' clothes; she had bought one or two off-the-peg designs before she was engaged.

Three months after her engagement was announced, Lady Diana's sister, Lady Jane, took her to see Donald Campbell at his William Street business in Knightsbridge. She was impressed, and it was his crepe-de-chine white dress and jacket decorated with floral sprigs which the new Princess wore on the first day of her honeymoon aboard *Britannia*. Two years later, in 1983, one of her favourite dresses was the fuchsia and white spotted silk dress he designed for her for the Australian tour.

Both Lady Jane and Lady Sarah, Diana's elder sisters, worked for Vogue before they were married, and it was through them that she was introduced to many more of London's leading designers. They were also responsible for putting her in touch with Vogue's senior fashion editor, Anna Harvey, who was, and still is, one of the Princess' most influential advisers. Apart from pointing out any suitable new designers who come on the scene and who can be visited by the Princess, Anna Harvey regularly collects a rail full of Britain's latest appropriate fashions and takes them to Kensington Palace, where the Princess can browse through them at her leisure. During her engagement Lady Diana went in person to Vogue to see the rail – her car could vanish quietly into Vogue House underground car park and the Princess-to-be could slip upstairs unnoticed. By and large the designs Anna Harvey chooses for the 'Royal Rail' are from off-the-peg warehouse designers, such as Jan Vanvelden, who do not design specifically for the Princess, and whose premises are not yet suitable for a Royal visit. Jan plans to invite the Princess to his Lexington Street, Soho, business when the stairwell has been 'done up'.

There aren't enough of Bill Pashley's clothes for them to be regularly loaded onto the Vogue rail. He designs, cuts and sews every piece of clothing by himself at his Battersea home. The personal touch is very obvious; the outfits he has designed for the Princess are similar to those she wore before her engagement, but they have that extra haute couture touch which takes them out of the ordinary and puts them in a class of their own. The Bill Pashley houndstooth check tweed suit the newly-wed Princess wore to a photo call at Balmoral was a case in point. Every country lady has a brown tweed suit, but here was one with a certain extra flair, from the jacket to the well-cut, front-pleat skirt. Bill Pashley was also responsible for the blue, green and white, flowery cotton skirt and waistcoat Lady Diana has worn to polo matches. It was so like the printed cottons she wore in her kindergarten teacher days, but the cut and the material showed that this was no off-the-peg, Laura Ashley type of ensemble.

Ascot Race Week, traditionally a grand fashion occasion, presented Lady Diana with an important testing ground for her fast-developing Royal dress sense. During Ascot Week she would rub shoulders with some of Britain's most fashionable women, so she couldn't afford to make any mistakes. One Ascot outfit came from her well-tried favourites, Bellville Sassoon, and for another she turned to David Neill who, with his partner Julia Fortescue, made a multi-coloured, striped silk three-piece, worn on several occasions since. They also designed the red silk dress patterned with stars which she first wore to Nicholas Soames' wedding. Lady Diana had come across David Neill designs through her Vogue magazine advisers, and it was they who introduced her to Gina Fratini's creations. The first one she saw was a cream organza ballgown which was lined up with several other sets of clothes, including an Emanuel blouse, for a Vogue personality sitting shot by Snowdon. For some of the pictures the Princess-to-be wore the ballgown – it suited her so well the designer gave it to her. Since then the Princess has worn a multi-coloured striped silk Gina Fratini on tour Down Under; one of her dramatic black velvet capes; a green velvet dress with a puritan collar and, most striking of all, a horizontally-striped taffeta evening dress with a strapless black velvet top, and a white silk and lace ball dress worn to the Trudeau dinner in Canada.

That Vogue personality sitting in November 1980 – before she was engaged to Prince Charles – had plenty of spin-offs. It was there that she first saw an Emanuel design – the pale pink blouse tied at the neck with a bow – which she wore for some of the Snowdon pictures. The blouse suited Lady Diana and, soon after the sitting, she went to see husband and wife David and Elizabeth Emanuel to buy some clothes for her new wardrobe. A few months later, after she had rifled through a few of London's foremost collections, the Princess returned to the Emanuel's in search of a dress to wear on her first formal engagement with Prince Charles; the evening at Goldsmiths Hall during which she met Princess Grace of Monaco. She spotted a low-cut, sequined, strapless black ball dress, and even in its unmade-up state Lady Diana set her heart on it. The effect was certainly dramatic, but the dress did not meet with universal approval – many felt it was simply too revealing for a future Princess.

Undaunted, the Princess kept up her search for a success formula for her new wardrobe, no doubt bolstered by stories of her great-grandfather, the sixth Earl Spencer, whose dress sense won nationwide admiration – so much so that he was universally known as a dandy and, when he died, many newspapers commented on the fact that he had always been renowned for his well-groomed appearance, "especially his exceptionally high collars and elaborate cravats". Lady Diana, too, made high collars famous; in her case pretty, lacy ones.

Already 'Lady Di' blouses run up by the mass market were selling like hot cakes, partly because they looked so pretty, partly because of their romantic associations. Another craze sparked off by Lady Diana's engagement was the 'Lady Di' hairstyle (the Di nickname has never been liked by the Princess, but made such useful headline shorthand that it soon became common currency) created by Kevin Shanley at the Chelsea salon Head Lines. Kevin, a good-looking, down-to-earth Londoner, was let into the secret of Lady Diana's engagement shortly before it was announced to the rest of the world. Since then he has followed the Princess around the world keeping her locks in order during tours. But in the months after the engagement Kevin had to think out how best to keep the character of his famous client's hair while at the same time cutting it to suit hats and tiaras. Kevin continued to streak and style Lady Diana's hair, but he let it grow – in some places to double its previous length, giving her a softer hairstyle which could be curled around hats and tiaras.

Lady Diana's new look was beginning to take shape. But, the future Princess decided, she would have to lose some weight before she could successfully wear many of the clothes which took her fancy in the designer showrooms and on the Vogue fashion rail. The willowy young lady could never be called fat or even plump – but she had slightly chubby cheeks and, perhaps, one or two pounds of puppy fat. With her usual single-minded determination Lady Diana cut out all the sweeties she so liked to munch in her bachelor-girl days and cut down on all the fatties' favourites like chocolate cake and lemon soufflé which she liked so much as a schoolgirl. On top of a sensible diet, Lady Diana started taking regular exercise. In Buckingham Palace she often made her way to the Palace pool to swim her way thinner, and, on some afternoons she would don a leotard and do an hour or more of tap dancing and ballet.

The regime worked wonders, and by the time of her wedding Lady Diana had slimmed from a size 12 to a size 10, and her plump cheeks had vanished to reveal high cheekbones, a good bone structure and an elfin-like face.

On duty, by the time of her wedding, Lady Diana could boast several fashion successes; she passed fashion-conscious Ascot Week with flying colours; she had been a hit on several daytime engagements – on visits to Cheltenham, Broadlands (the home of the late Lord Mountbatten, Prince Charles' honorary grandfather) and to her future home town, Tetbury, Gloucestershire. And by later examining the Press and TV reports and pictures of herself, the Princess-to-be was fast learning from her mistakes. The slightly too matronly clothes which she wore for her first on-duty appearances – chosen because they seemed formal and correct – were being replaced by younger styles still completely in keeping with her new job. But off duty at polo matches and race meetings, where the Princess was still photographed by the world Press, Lady Diana wasn't doing so well. Her jeans and her dungarees were too casual, even for an off-duty Royal fiancée. It was on such occasions that she wore all her old bachelor-day favourites from chain stores such as Benetton. Inca and Brother Sun were also sources of such clothes (although she still uses most of these shops she buys a different style of clothes and now wears them with more panache). As she learned more about fashion possibilities the Princess, who has always been interested in clothes, started to dress with casual chic. Dungarees and jeans were swapped for cool, candy-striped pale blue and white striped trousers with a silk shirt, or smart pedal pushers. The clothes were casual, comfortable and attractive without being too informal.

But the dramatic changes in her off-duty wardrobe did not come until after Lady Diana was married. She could hardly be expected to pay much attention to her informal wardrobe. Wedding preparations took up most of her time. Most important of all, she was going to regular fittings for The Dress. Press speculation as to who might design the wedding dress began almost as soon as the wedding announcement was made – and artists' impressions of what X designer or Y designer might create for Lady Diana if asked, were published over plenty of fashion pages. Lady Diana had, however, made up her mind early on, and she turned to David and Elizabeth Emanuel, the people who had made her black ballgown, to make her a wedding dress. David, a dapper, charming blond, and his wife Elizabeth – petite, dark-haired and bubbly, are an amiable couple, and more important, their style was just the thing for a beautiful young princess-to-be. The crinolined, tight-waisted wedding dresses in silk and lace decorated with bows which Emanuel had made for past weddings were ideal for a fairy-tale princess.

There were fashion and newspaper editors all over the world who would have given a great deal to know what The Dress looked like, and so while Dorset silkworms munched mulberry leaves overtime to produce thousands of feet of thread for the wedding dress taffeta, the Emanuels had to work as hard on security as on the dress design to prevent a whisper about The Dress getting outside their salon. Only their most trusted employees were allowed near the bride's and bridesmaids' dresses; blinds appeared in the upstairs windows where the dresses were being made; a safe was installed; every piece of excess fabric was burned rather than being thrown in the bins which had been known to disappear mysteriously, and the Emanuels learned overnight how to avoid sticky questions from the Press who had surrounded their workrooms.

Their careful security was well worthwhile – one picture purporting to be an exact copy of the Princess' dress appeared a day or so before the wedding – but it was nowhere near the real thing. At ten-thirty on July 29th, 1981, Lady Diana climbed into the Glass Coach at Clarence House – and for the first time the wedding dress went on public display. At St Paul's, when the Princess-to-be stepped out of the carriage, her crinolined dress, fluttering veil and 25-foot train floating around her, Liz Emanuel's vision of the Royal bride looking like a butterfly breaking out of its chrysalis took shape. Light shimmered and danced off the dress and veil which was spangled with thousands of pearl sequins, and the lace ruffles and flounces at the collar of the dress made a perfect frame for the bride's face. Sadly, in the cramped carriage which carried Lady Diana and her father Earl Spencer, the wedding dress became a little crumpled – but the dress was not the disaster some commentators liked to make it. "Too fussy", they said, "the sleeves are too big", said others, while others still said the ivory silk was the wrong colour for the Princess. But in the Cathedral from my seat behind the Spencer family, the dress was perfect. Anything more simple would have looked stark and boring in the lavish cathedral surroundings, and the massive sleeves and great ruffles around the neck emphasised the bride's tiny waist and long neck.

With her wedding and honeymoon behind her, the new Princess of Wales could settle down to her new job, and work out exactly what kind of Princess she was going to be. First, of course, there were the clothes. Bellville Sassoon's clothes had hit just the right note of pretty elegance during the engagement and there was no reason they shouldn't do the same now. When the Princess discovered that she was pregnant, it was Bellville Sassoon she first asked to make some maternity clothes. Then she turned to Jan Vanvelden, a designer she had never before used, and asked him to adjust some of the clothes she had spotted from his label. Jan comes from a very different background from that of Bellville Sassoon. He is the 41-year-old eldest son of a grand sweet shop owner and baker – the equivalent of Floris – in Amsterdam, and made his name as a designer in his own right only two years ago, after leaving his previous designer firm in London. Belinda Bellville on the other hand is the grand-daughter of Cuckoo Leith, who was an important name in the dress world of the 1920s, and her partner David Sassoon was trained at the Royal College of Art.

Gina Fratini is in a different mould again, and while David Sassoon and Jan Vanvelden wear casual, informal clothes, Gina – a distinguished, grey-haired lady – wears classic, formal designs. She has, like so many of the Princess' designers, a genuine and seemingly boundless enthusiasm for the Princess' looks. "She really is so lovely, isn't she", said Gina, leafing through some photographs of her Royal client. "She looks good in every single picture." She too, along with Caroline Charles, David Neill, Bruce Oldfield and Jasper Conran was asked to make maternity clothes for the Princess. Jasper, just a year older than the Princess, is the son of Terence the designer, and author Shirley of *Superwoman* fame. Bruce Oldfield, who is half-Jamaican, is another young designer – only eleven years older than the Princess. In the early months of her pregnancy the Princess wore one of Bruce Oldfield's outfits, in blue velvet, when she turned on the Christmas lights in Regent Street, London.

One of the Princess' more recent discoveries in the designer world is Hachi, the London-based Japanese designer. It was a strange fluke of fate which brought Hachi, a round-faced, quiet man, to this country. As an up-and-coming young designer in Japan he had set his heart on going to New York – but his parents forbade him, saying it was too dangerous. Instead he came to London and set up a salon just off Bond Street. The most striking Hachi dress worn so far by the Princess is a clinging, crepe-de-chine silk, one-shouldered dress embroidered with crystal beads. The first time the Princess wore it in public – on the last night of her Australian tour – the dress took even one of her staff by surprise. Goggle-eyed, he managed to splutter, "She looks *fantastic*. I mean she always looks good but this is amazing." The clinging lines of Hachi's dress certainly show off the Princess' well-toned, trim figure – and the silvery light thrown off by the crystal beads give her an almost other-worldly quality.

In her engagement months, when the Princess-to-be was still finding her feet in the fashion world, she went almost exclusively to designers for her formal working wardrobe. But since her marriage she has branched out and now regularly uses ready-to-wear fashions. Roland Klein's firm Marcel Fenez has supplied the Princess with suits and dresses, and from Jaeger's she bought the burgundy embroidered suit worn during the tour of Wales soon after her honeymoon.

Her shoe stockists though have remained largely the same designers and firms today as they were before the wedding. Her wedding shoes were made by Clive Shilton but Zapata, Jourdan and The Chelsea Cobbler have supplied footwear for the Princess over the past three years and she has had shoes made by Edward Rayne, the Queen's shoemakers, and by Manolo Blahnik. The Princess takes a generous size 6 and rarely agrees to heels over two inches high – otherwise she towers over the Prince.

But the Princess' fashions are only one part of her fashion story. Before the wedding bells had sounded, the Prince's wardrobe had been given a touch of Lady Diana magic. From the time it was clear that theirs was a serious romance, Lady Diana started to buy one or two things for her loved one's wardrobe. One of her major and most surprising breakthroughs came early on when she presented the Prince with a pair of slip-on shoes. Much to everyone's amazement he seemed happy to abandon his deeply traditional lace-ups and wear the newfangled slip-ons from time to time. And it wasn't even as if they were hand made by Lobbs, like all the rest of his shoes! Her next onslaught on the Royal wardrobe came in the shape of some shirts and ties from the Prince's shirtmakers Turnball and Asser. Unlike his usual cautious choice of shirts which rarely ventured outside the plain white traditional style, these shirts had stripes...and the ties were quite colourful compared with many the Prince wore. There were jumpers as well – none of them as outrageous as the koala jumper she wore stretched over her tummy when she was pregnant. All the same, the clothes were a departure from his normal style. But probably her greatest triumph came when the Prince had three smart, double-breasted suits made. The dark, elegant suits were a far cry from his single-breasted suits.

Over the years the Prince had got used to wearing a certain style of 'mufti' made by Johns and Pegg. It was similar in cut to his uniforms – but not as flattering. Until the Princess arrived on the scene no one had persuaded the Prince to experiment with his fashions – and the problem was made worse because the Prince left long intervals between buying new suits. Thus they became dated, and started to sag and bag despite constant and careful attention from his staff. Prince Charles' bachelor-days wardrobe had not been a good advertisement for British tailoring – through no fault of the bespoke British tailors involved. The Princess soon changed that, and, to complete the Prince's dapper new look, he took to wearing buttonholes far more often than he had in the past.

Some of those following Prince Charles have wondered aloud why the Prince decided not to wear jeans when he attended a 1982 Status Quo concert in Birmingham. The truth is that, as he himself pointed out, he is not a trendy person and jeans, however suitable for the occasion, would simply have looked rather silly on the heir to the throne. The Princess, more than anyone, knows exactly where to draw the line between smartening up the Prince's wardrobe and making him wear unsuitable clothes – which is why he so readily agreed to the changes she suggested.

The year 1981 was a heady one for 19-year-old Lady Diana, who turned into the 20-year-old Princess of Wales. She became a wife, a Princess, a fashion leader for the world, a Royal celebrity and, on top of it all, she found herself Mistress of Highgrove House, the couple's Gloucestershire retreat, their flat in Kensington Palace and a set of rooms in Windsor Castle. She sailed into her new responsibilities with apparent confidence. Before starting on the run-of-the-mill, daily life at their residences the Princess set to work with the interior designer Dudley Poplak making her new homes cosy and pretty. The hall at Highgrove sets the mood for the rest of the house. It is rag-rolled – a laborious technique which gives a blotchy-marbled effect – in coral pink.

The same colour, just a little paler, dominates the couple's bedroom, which has matching floral drapes around the windows and four-poster. There are four reception rooms – her sitting room is warm yellow, the drawing room is green with magnificent fringed curtains caught in drapes, and the dining room is a slightly darker green. Upstairs there are nine bedrooms, five of them with dressing rooms, a nursery wing and servants' wing. There are also no less than six bathrooms. Even so, by Royal standards Highgrove is not big, and in the future it may prove to be too small for the family. But it is a pretty, eighteenth-century Cotswold stone building set in 348 acres of rolling countryside not far from Princess Anne and her family. When Lady Diana first saw the house the only habitable rooms were a few bedrooms in which Charles, his detective and valet would 'camp' on off-duty weekends. It must have been a daunting sight to Prince Charles' future wife, used as she was to the comfort of her own prettily-furnished London flat or her father's palatial stately home, Althorp.

The second project – also tackled jointly by the Princess and Dudley Poplak – were Kensington Palace apartment numbers eight and nine, set aside for the Royal couple. The apartments are on three floors, and some of the staff rooms are interspersed with offices. The nanny's quarters, along with the playroom and the night nursery, are on the top floor, above the Royal bedroom, and there is a barbecue on the roof. There is a sitting room for the Princess, a music room and adjoining breakfast room, two guest rooms and several bathrooms. Outside there is a helicopter pad. The décor is very similar to that at Highgrove, the Princess' sitting room in particular has a slightly Laura Ashley feel to it, with pinkish-pastelly prints abounding. Once again, space may prove to be a problem for the new family at their London home.

Lady Diana turned Princess of Wales got off to a fine start in her first Royal year – but there were storm clouds on the horizon. Trouble began a month or so after Prince William was born amid great national rejoicing. The Princess returned to London from the annual Royal holiday at Balmoral earlier than expected, and embarked on a series of shopping sprees while the Prince remained in Scotland. Nothing could be more understandable – the Princess, having worked hard to regain her sylph-like, pre-pregnancy figure, could hardly wait to get into all the latest fashions. But there were those who said that her marriage was veering towards the rocks, and that she was a 'shopaholic'. The gossip and rumours must have wounded the young couple but there was little they could do. Matters came to a head on a skiing holiday in the New Year when, despite pleas from Prince Charles, the Princess refused to co-operate for photographers – the idea being that if the photographers got the pictures they needed they, and the reporters, would leave the Royal couple in peace for the rest of the holiday. In the past Prince Charles had normally agreed to such an arrangement – but the Princess decided to put her foot down – this was a private holiday, and that's how she intended to keep it. Ugly headlines recorded the incident at home and some called the Princess 'spoilt' – but in the end she won the day – no one got any clear photographs of her on her skiing holiday.

Seven weeks later Diana was once again the darling of the Press. The young wife, mother and Princess was finally to prove herself in the eyes of the world when she set off on a gruelling tour of Australia and New Zealand. Once more the Princess' common-sense approach to life won the day – and in the same way that she had decided against having Prince William at Buckingham Palace and opted instead to go along with the wishes of her gynaecologist and have her baby in hospital, so the Princess decided to break another tradition and take Prince William with her on tour. The Queen had already relaxed her rule that those in direct line to the throne should not travel together – but it came as a surprise that she allowed both Prince Charles and Prince William to make the long air journey together from Heathrow to Alice Springs and then across to New Zealand. The Princess was determined to prove that she could be a good mother, wife and Princess; was determined to prove that having a good family life did not rule out having a full working life as a Royal. It took someone with the Princess' courage to carry out her convictions.

No doubt the Princess' nerves were on edge as she and the Prince walked down the steps from the Royal Australian Air Force Boeing at Alice Springs, the starting point of their Australian tour in 1983. She had been put through a baptism of fire by Press and public in Britain, but now she had to face her first-ever tour. She knew that from the moment the Boeing door opened and she faced the blazing outback heat her every movement, her every word and expression, her every piece of clothing, would be scrutinised by an eager public Down Under and at home, and be reported on and recorded by the hundreds of Press, TV and radio men and women who would follow her on that six-week trial.

That first day there were some people in the crowd at Alice Springs airport who had driven hundreds of miles through the dusty red outback to catch a glimpse of the legend of which they had heard and read so much – and they were not disappointed. As the crowds pressed forward to see her and thrust flowers into her hands she managed to talk to a few, shake hands with others and smile at them all – she had in that first twenty minutes begun to weave her spell, and she left the crowd entranced. There were some there who, as we asked what the Princess had said to them and what they thought of her, were still so overcome by their Royal encounter that they could only gasp "she...she *talked* to me...she's...she's...*gorgeous*" or "her skin...it's...it's beautiful and soft". And when asked what the Princess had said to them "she...she...said 'Hi'". From there the party travelled to the seat of the new Government in Canberra, where, thought some gloomy members of the Royal party, the people might not welcome the Royal couple – after all, a Republican Government had recently been voted into office – but adoring or curious thousands crammed into city centres and parks to see the Royal couple. Infuriated Republican sympathisers wrote that the police must have done something rather nasty to keep Republican supporters from demonstrating. They hadn't – most Australians just couldn't get enough of their Royal visitors – and especially of the beautiful young Princess. The same high fervour greeted the Prince and Princess' visit to New Zealand, and although the weather turned chilly the crowds still turned out in their thousands, sometimes waiting for hours in the hope of catching a glimpse of them. There, the cry was "Oh!...she's *beautiful*". And as her confidence grew, the Princess – impossible though it might have seemed – acquired an extra glow.

By the time the Princess' trunks were packed for the Royal couple's second tour that year – this time to Canada – her style had reached a new peak. Her working confidence was such that Prince Charles no longer felt the need to glance over his shoulder to see how she was managing on walkabouts, and while in Canada she told one of her hosts that she had at last begun to feel "like a real Princess". Her clothes had acquired a new touch of elegance, typified by Jasper Conran's simple-lined suits in bright blocks of colour. But even today she hasn't sacrificed her much-loved 'Lady Di' look for her new elegance, and still wears many blouses, pieces of jewellery and dresses similar to those she wore before her wedding. Necklines have always been one of the Princess' specialities and she still wears a wide variety of striking collars, from flouncy, ruffled, butterfly and lacy necklines to plainer, shirt collar styles. She has also retained her flair for wearing blouses that give her a soft, filmy look similar to that in the Snowdon pictures taken before her wedding. And, of course, she still wears multi-stranded pearl chokers, which sparked off a craze for such jewellery soon after her engagement was announced.

Both tours were a huge success in every respect, and the Australian tour in particular exceeded the Royal entourage's greatest expectations. The Queen was delighted and sent messages of congratulations to the Prince and Princess. The Press was delighted because it could write happy stories for once; and the Princess was happy because she had made everyone else happy; from old people in wheelchairs to little children clutching bunches of flowers; from teenagers to Prime Ministers; from Presidents to policemen and women holding back enthusiastic crowds, the Princess charmed them all. They liked her pretty clothes, her simple way of talking to everyone, her distinctly friendly manner and her big smile.

A few years back Princess Alexandra said, "Nowadays we have to compete with Elizabeth Taylor and the Beatles". Today there is no competition – the Princess is in another league. And the key to her popularity and her success as a Royal is her style. Her clothes are now Royal without being boring or frumpy; she has that indefinable aura of being Royal and yet she is never too grand for mischievous, sticky-fingered children. She has in three years become a Royal, a wife and a mother and one of the world's most photographed and best-loved young ladies.

'If this set of pictures arrived on my desk,' said one of the Princess' designers, 'I would try to hire the Princess to model my clothes. She is as perfect as a fashion plate – tall, slim and pretty. She has done so much for British fashion.' Here the Princess is at a polo match wearing the black and white Jan Vanvelden blouse and black leather cummerbund originally designed with a black skirt for an Adelaide students' dance.

From State banquets to film premieres, the Princess is always the belle of the ball. Her ever-pretty, ever-royal clothes (opposite, a Chelsea Design Company dress) matched with that smile make the Princess a show stopper.

John Boyd, the Princess' hatter, had a surprise when the Princess was preparing her wardrobe for the Braemar Games. She arrived at John Boyd's shop with one of Prince Charles' tam-o-shanters – and asked for a copy for herself. The Scottish hatter was a little taken aback – a 'tammy' wasn't his usual style. On the other hand women have worn tammies in the past – so the Princess got hers with John Boyd's blessing.

At last she had married her
Prince, and now the new
Princess could look forward to
a honeymoon away from it all.
After a lavish wedding
reception at Buckingham Palace
the couple spent a few days at
the late Earl Mountbatten's
home, Broadlands, and then
cruised the Greek islands in
*Britannia*.

Princess Pensive ...the Princess snatched a few seconds on
the hectic Canadian tour possibly to think about Prince
William left behind at home.

The epitome of casual chic, the Princess wore grey pedal pushers (far right top) with a white frilly blouse, red pullover and matching red leather cummerbund to a polo match in the summer of 1983. In her engagement days Lady Diana used to pull on a pair of dungarees to watch polo. Since her wedding the Princess has worked as hard on her 'off duty' wardrobe as her working one. On the opposite page the Princess is wearing a shimmering silk chiffon pastel dress by Belville Sassoon, bought during her engagement.

Signs that the Princess was expecting her first baby in the summer of 1982 didn't stop the fashion-conscious young lady from looking her best. That winter colourful, fluffy coats kept her warm and fashionable. Cut on a wide 'A' line, or with generous gathers falling from a yoke, the coats made cosy Royal maternity wear.

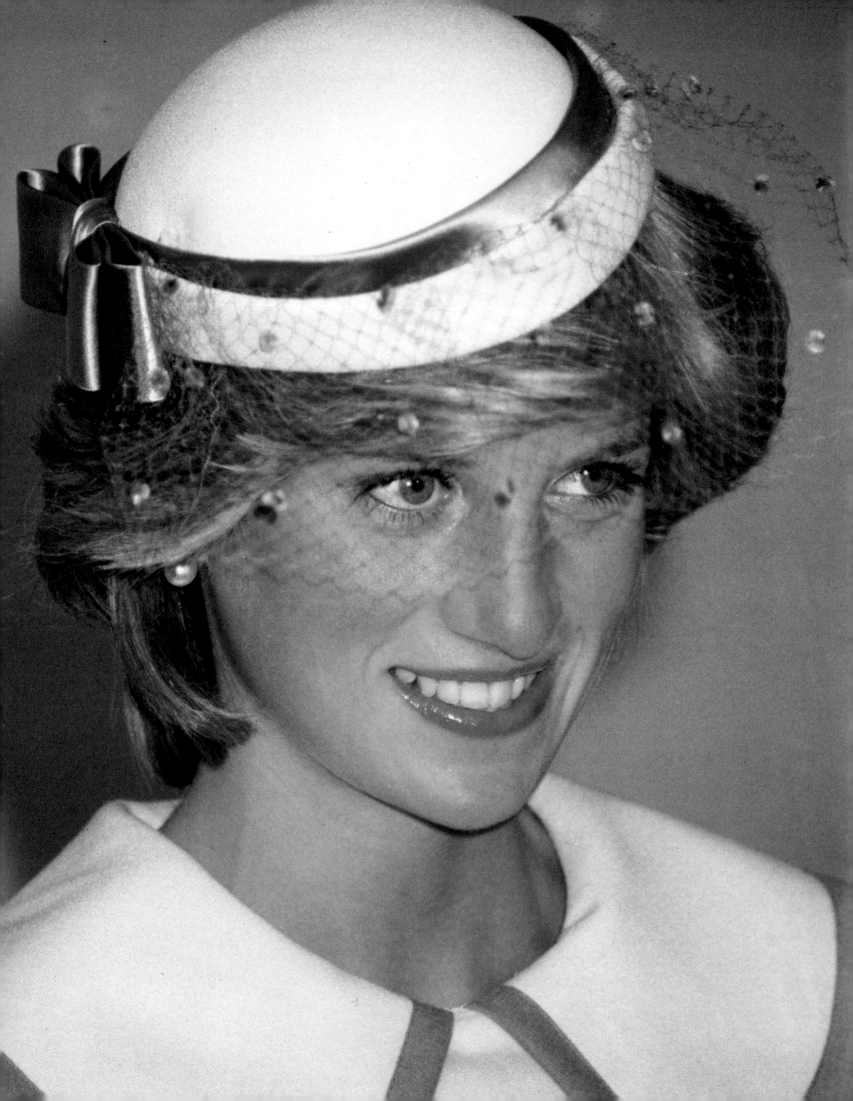

Whites and off-whites and the palest pastels help show off the Princess' peaches and cream complexion, although in Ottawa she told admirers who asked that grey was one of her favourite colours – she wore a grey dress that day.

Veiled hats are Prince Charles' favourites – they show off his wife's large blue eyes. But dainty little veils like the ones above and left look Spartan beside the Royal wedding veil, spangled with hundreds of pearl sequins.

Roars of approval greeted the Princess-to-be as her carriage trundled from Clarence House to St Paul's Cathedral, and an estimated 750 million people around the world were spellbound. Inside the Cathedral, at the first rustles of her silk and lace crinoline dress by the Emanuels, a hush fell over the congregation and the ceremony began. Later Prince Andrew injected a little mischief into the proceedings. He tied silver and blue gas balloons and a 'Just Married' sign on the back of his big brother's going away carriage.

In Australia (above) the Princess received, besides flowers, a tiny Aboriginal boomerang for Prince William.

Down Under on tour the Princess – 'Liedy Doi' – was everywhere greeted by ecstatic devotees. When she spotted this enterprising youngster crawling to the front of the crowd on his hands and knees with a bunch of daisies for her, she bent to take them and give him a special 'thankyou'.

Royal carriages are not normally like the wild west style coach (facing page). When the Prince and Princess visited Sovereign Hill historical park in Victoria, Australia, the Royal couple gamely climbed aboard for a bumpy twenty minute ride.

Evening dresses can be quite a problem for Royal ladies. They have to stand out but cannot be outrageous; they have to look glamorous but not risque; pretty without being fussy. The Princess tackled the problem with her usual panache, and from her pre-wedding styles like the revealing diamante-strap dress (left) she turned to dresses such as the blue and silver Bruce Oldfield creation (right).

The wedding dress was made with OLD lace, NEW silk spun by silkworms in Dorset; the tiara was BORROWED from the Spencer family collection, and a tiny BLUE bow was sewn into the waistband.

Salmon pink silk was turned into the dress and jacket (left) for the Princess' going away outfit. Belville Sassoon designed it, and since then the Princess has worn it many times. The little-girl style was a far cry from the almost

austere, elegant red suit by Jasper Conran (below) the Princess wore in Shelburne, Canada, or the sophisticated, drop-waisted, one-shoulder dress (right). While in Shelburne the Prince and Princess visited the Dory Shop

- a dory is a fishing boat – where they were given a model of a dory for Prince William of Wales. For the Prince and Princess themselves there was an eighteenth century Loyalist Doll – for the couple were visiting a Loyalist stronghold.

It was during the Prince and Princess' Canadian tour that the Royal yacht *Britannia* had to manoeuvre past three large blue-green icebergs to get into St John's Harbour. It was the first time the Princess of Wales had seen an iceberg: she was fascinated.

No, the Princess hadn't dyed her hair orange, and turned punk for an engagement! The temporary new hair colour came from the Regent St Christmas lights which the Princess had just switched on (below right). It was one of the earliest solo engagements of her Royal career, and she seemed to enjoy herself. 'I've brought my old man, where's yours?' asked fellow guest Cilla Black. 'I left him at home watching the telly,' the Princess replied.

As Duchess of Cornwall the Princess was given a special welcome when she visited St

Columb, where townsfolk were celebrating the 650th anniversary of their charter from King Edward III. The Royal couple opted to travel in an open car – but a chill in the air decided the Princess to wear a fine wool suit. This time she wore it with a high lacy collar peeping over the Cossack-style neckline, but a few months earlier (left) she wore it on its own. Necklines are one of the Princess' specialities.

The Jan Vanvelden shirt (left) was designed with a tie – but the Princess wore it without. That afternoon, on tour Down Under, the Princess' ensemble was one of the few diverting sights. The engagement was a fire fighting display.

Security is always a headache, and Royal detectives have to learn to blend into their surroundings while keeping close to their charges. Pictured (far left) is the Princess of Wales in New Zealand wearing a lilac evening dress – one of her detectives is in the background, in dinner suit. But whatever the occasion and whatever the clothes they have to wear, Royal detectives are always armed.

It was an historic moment when the Princess emerged from St Mary's Hospital, Paddington to give her first baby, Prince William of Wales, his first public airing. Waiting crowds of wellwishers and Press shared the joyful moment with the Prince and Princess before the Royal couple drove home to Kensington Palace. What a difference from Prince Charles' birth in the privacy and seclusion of Buckingham Palace.

Victor Edelstein's pink evening dress (above) was first worn by the Princess in Australia when a young pianist sang a song specially written for her.

Dress for the barbeque (far right) thrown by Prime Minister Trudeau near Ottawa was informal. Photographers wondered aloud if the Princess would turn up wearing jeans and a check shirt...but instead she chose to wear a blue cotton Arabella Pollen sailor dress. Steaks sizzled on the open air grills – but the Prince and Princess opted for salmon.

In Tasmania on the first Royal tour, the weather turned quite chilly, and it was a surprise to see the Princess in the cool, red and white linen suit by Belville Sassoon (right). In New Zealand the weather was even colder – so much so that a collection of warmer clothes had to be ordered, made and flown from England post haste.

Green may be unlucky for some, but the Princess is the exception to prove the rule. Left to right – at home in England soon after her engagement; a green and white dress on tour Down Under; and in Canada a green Jasper Conran suit which is the epitome of style. If she wears green for the evening the Princess swaps her favourite stones, sapphires, for emeralds. When it came to the day when Prince William gave his first photo call in New Zealand the Princess once more opted for green.

The joyful news that the Princess was expecting her first baby posed the usual practical problem for any mum-to-be. The Princess turned to Jan Vanvelden and asked him to modify one of his red and white striped dresses (below).

The Jan Vanvelden maternity clothes were such a success the Princess kept the designer busy after her baby arrived, and he made her clothes like the red and white two piece pictured right. Flamboyant collars suit the Princess. (Facing page) she is wearing a clown collar over a gabardine suit by Jasper Conran.

Teddy was given to the Princess while she was visiting Canterbury – her smile shows how much she liked the large cuddly bear. But it is unlikely to have found its way to Prince William's nursery. Most of the thousands

embroidered with thousands of crystal beads made the Princess' Hachi dress (opposite) one of the most successful evening dresses on tour in Australia. She wore it on her last night out there; it made a stunning finale.

of gifts showered on the Royal Family every year are given to children's hospitals or charities. Even so, everyone who gives something to a member of the Royal Family gets a letter of thanks from a member of the Household – so long as a name and address has been attached.

Clinging silk crepe

Prince Charles' fiancée Lady Diana Spencer visited Earl Mountbatten's home Broadlands in May 1981. The pretty but chubby cheeked young lady was just beginning her Royal career – two years later, as the pictures on the rest of this page show, the Princess was transformed. Her face was thinner, her figure so trim that some worried that she might have the slimmer's disease anorexia.

Anne Bolton, one of Lady Diana's flatmates in her bachelor girl days, met up with the Princess at a polo match in Australia and let her into the secret of her new romance. Five months later Anne announced her engagement to Noel Hill, son of Prince Charles' close friend and polo advisor Sinclair Hill. While living in Australia Anne developed a flamboyant Antipodean dress style. The Princess stuck to her demure style that day with a Chelsea Design Company sailor dress.

Klondike style clothes were the order of the day when the Princess and the Prince visited a reconstruction of a gold rush town in Canada. The cream bustle dress under which

large pink bow made for the same tour, and worn many times subsequently. On the day the Princess wore the clown suit she watched a keep fit class at Adelaide Community Centre.

dainty kidskin lace-up boots peeped scored a hit with the barbeque hosts that night. So did Prince Charles' outfit – a frock coat, cravat and wing collar.

Arabella Pollen made the

striped silk clown suit pictured above left. The Princess wore it once in Australia – but the suit wasn't as much of a success as the same designer's blue sailor suit trimmed with a

As Earl Spencer walked down the aisle of St Paul's he must have been the proudest man in the land – even when Lady Diana muddled her future husband's names. 'She's just married my father!' exclaimed Prince Andrew.

During a Press reception held by the Royal couple at Alice Springs, the Princess wore the white silk suit decorated with flower sprigs which she first wore for her honeymoon. The next day she went for a more formal style with the yellow silk Jan Vanvelden dress (bottom left). But for the Royal visit to Ayers Rock the Princess decided on an informal Benny Ong dress (right). And while some of us sweltered in the heat the Princess looked remarkably cool.

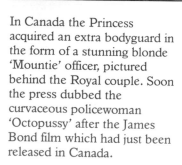

In Canada the Princess acquired an extra bodyguard in the form of a stunning blonde 'Mountie' officer, pictured behind the Royal couple. Soon the press dubbed the curvaceous policewoman 'Octopussy' after the James Bond film which had just been released in Canada.

In Australia the Princess was looked after by a different plain clothes policewoman in every state – to the delight of the Press they were all good looking. In the Northern Territory the elegant detective looking after the Princess kept her gun down the front of her dress!

David Sassoon made the cosy blue coat (bottom left) – the gathered front made it an ideal maternity cover up. Later, on tour in Canada the Princess pulled on a rather sombre raincoat while the Prince donned his Burberry to keep out the rain. A far cry from her blue coat – but they were determined the rain wouldn't make any difference to their schedule.

It was Easter Sunday in the quiet little town of Albury, New South Wales – and for once the place was thronging with crowds, out to see the Princess and the Prince. At first she appeared to be wearing a new ensemble – in fact it was a combination of an 'old' Miss Antonette quilted jacket over the blue green dress she wore at the start of the Australian tour.

Murray Arbeid made the deep yellow taffeta dress (left) the Princess wore for dinner at Government House, Canberra after a day spent with the Prime Minister. She and Prince Charles won the hearts of Mr and Mrs Hawke and many other republicans. That night, decked out in the glittering diamond Family Order brooch decorated with a portrait of Her Majesty The Queen, the Princess knew she had cleared yet another Royal hurdle.

The Princess appeared a little embarrassed by the Maori jade fertility symbol which was hung round her neck at Waitangi, New Zealand, and tried to keep it covered with a bunch of yellow flowers.

variety concert in Melbourne, Victoria. And the silk crepe day dress with matching jacket was just the right combination of bright colour and sophistication for Sydney, New South Wales. The crowds waiting for the Royal couple in Sydney turned the Opera House steps into a cheering mass of humanity. So many

The bright red strapless dress with a lacy jacket was made by Jan Vanvelden. The Princess wore it on the eve of her 22nd birthday at a Government House dinner in Edmonton, Canada. A Welsh male voice choir

entertained the Royal couple. Both pink dresses are by the Chelsea Design Company. The gold and pink sari silk dress which rustled provocatively with the sound of petticoats, was just the thing for a

people turned out for 'Chas and Di' that the half mile Royal journey from the Opera House to Parliament House became almost impossible.

Natural fabrics are usually the only materials the Princess of Wales will wear. By their very nature the fabrics crease easily, and so a lady's maid is almost

Like the Queen Mother the Princess has a natural and charming smile which radiates warmth and happiness. In the days leading up to her wedding, when Lady Diana

Spencer covered a few engagements, she would often blush and turn away from the cameras when she smiled – almost as if she were embarrassed by her display of

indispensable, especially during whistle stop tours when trunks of silks, cottons and wools have to be unpacked and reloaded almost every night. The maids responsible for having the clothes ready and pressed were Valerie Gibbs in Australia and Canada, and Evelyn Dagley in New Zealand.

happiness. The habit earned her the label 'shy Di' which has since proved to be wildly inaccurate. A retiring type would never have been able to cope with the Princess' work.

In a rare, off-guard moment Lady Diana Spencer tosses back her world-famous hairstyle (centre picture). That day The newly-engaged Lady Diana and Prince Charles visited Dean Close School in Cheltenham where an 18-year-old schoolboy, Nicholas Hardy asked: 'May I kiss the hand of my future Queen?' To his delight the future Princess smiled and replied, 'Yes, you may.' and Nicholas kissed Lady Diana's hand. As he did so Lady Diana couldn't help giving a girlish giggle and telling Nicholas 'You will never live this down.'

Tanned and relaxed, the Royal newly-weds returned from their honeymoon aboard *Britannia* and agreed to pose for photographs. Weeks later the Princess saw her gynaecologist Mr George Pinker. The joyful news was soon announced that the Princess was expecting her

first baby.

Women are fascinated by the Princess because her clothes are pretty, men adore her because she is pretty – and children love her because she is natural with them.

The blue and silver ruffled chiffon evening dress (above)

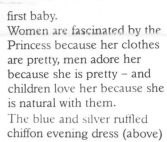

by Bruce Oldfield ensured the Princess was the belle of the ball in Sydney. The Royal couple opened the dancing at the Wentworth Hotel Charity Ball that March evening. Prince Charles' dancing was so fast and enthusiastic that the Princess had a mild fit of the giggles as she was whirled around the dance floor.

'LD' said the Princess' programme on April 18th 1983. That meant a Long Dress was to be worn to the New Zealand Ballet's *Coppelia*. The Princess wore an off-the-shoulder lilac silk dress.

Earlier for that day the Royal programme read DD or Day Dress for a visit to a display by local schoolchildren at Eden Park, Auckland. The Princess' DD was green and white silk.

Before her engagement Lady Diana Spencer played a game of cat and mouse with reporters and photographers. Sometimes it ended in tears, other times, as above, Lady Diana laughed it off. After her marriage Press relations improved and the Princess could relax. (Left) she is wearing a multi-coloured David Sassoon coat.

Keeping hats on the Princess' pretty head is a headache for her hatter John Boyd. While making a peach hat for her going away outfit one of John's employees remembered that her old hats had springs sewn into the brim to keep it

secure. A spring was found, dyed blond like the Princess' hair and popped into the brim, and, hey presto! the hat stayed on the Royal head. But sometimes the Princess still resorts to hatpins.

If Prince William proved anything during his first-ever Press call at Government House in New Zealand, it was that he isn't camera shy. Faced with a host of cameras the little Prince happily set off in their direction.

Lady Diana sometimes found the pressures hard to bear (right) – especially when she had to keep her feelings secret in the face of speculation about her relationship with Prince Charles. But on her first formal engagement when she wore the famous low-cut Emanuel dress the Princess-to-be had thrown off all her pre-engagement cares.

John Boyd's hats often make all the difference to an outfit. (Facing page) the beige beret gave the Princess of Wales' wool and black leather trim coat dress a

jaunty air while the brown brimmed hat gave a more demure air. Jasper Conran, who made the grey outfit, was misquoted in one upper-crust British magazine as complaining he didn't like his clothes being worn with 'Those Hats.' The magazine published an apology and the Princess continued to dress like a fashion plate... frequently wearing Jasper Conran's clothes and John Boyd's hats!

The Princess has quickly become a leading and invaluable member of 'The Firm' as Prince Charles' grandfather King George VI called the monarchy. Whether at the State Opening of Parliament (below), on tour (right) or at the Baemar Games in Scotland (far right) she is often the centre of attention. Behind the scenes too the Princess is hard at work helping one of her charities.

Photographer Tim Graham was asked by the Princess to take this official picture of little Prince William of Wales (facing page).

Dressed in the Honiton lace Christening robe first used for Queen Victoria's eldest child Princess Victoria, Prince William whimpered until the Princess gave him the comfort of her finger. Princess Victoria's Christening in 1841 set the precedent for generations of

Whereas little Vicky's Christening took place in the Chapel Royal, St James, William's was held at Buckingham Palace.

the Royal Family. Like her, Prince William was Christened in a font decorated with the Royal arms and designed by Prince Albert.

Thousands of children were 'bussed' into Newcastle, New South Wales, to sing for the Royal couple. Wearing a candy-striped dress by Chelsea Design Company and a matching jacket the Princess stayed far longer than planned.

A long flight from London to Alice Springs didn't seem to have had any effect on the Princess of Wales as she stood on the runway holding Prince William in her arms (right) on Sunday March 20th 1983. There were beds on the Royal couple's Royal Australian Air Force Boeing 707, and a sky cot for the baby Prince. Even so, the Princess embarked on her gruelling round of engagements that afternoon with remarkable stamina. Prince William was flown to his home-from-home, Woomargama in New South Wales.

Polo, said a critic of Lady Diana Spencer, was anathema to the Prince's girlfriend 'Lady Di'. That meant a heavy minus against her name in the marriage stakes – after all polo is one of the Prince's favourite sports. But the Princess loyally turned up to as many matches as her time allowed – even when she was pregnant (bottom left). The picture (below left) shows the Princess at polo a year later.

The Princess' natural elegance is heightened by this cool grey silk Jasper Conran two piece suit (right). The hazy outline of her slim legs gave the Princess of Wales a film star look which must have delighted the Prince.

The blue and while silk dress with contrast bodice appeared on tour Down Under and at a Dorchester reception (right). It helped the designer, Donald Campbell, acquire a Royal reputation.

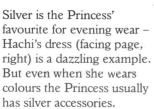

Silver is the Princess' favourite for evening wear – Hachi's dress (facing page, right) is a dazzling example. But even when she wears colours the Princess usually has silver accessories.

The Royal newlyweds had messages of good luck from around the world – but just in case, a tiny 18-carat yellow gold horseshoe studded with diamonds was sewn into the bride's dress. Every last detail had been covered, including the possibility of rain. The bridal gown designers, Emanuel, made a wedding umbrella of silk and lace embroidered with pearls and sequins. But the bride's silk slippers would not have fared well in the rain.

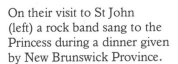

On their visit to St John (left) a rock band sang to the Princess during a dinner given by New Brunswick Province.

If the waiting crowds could put up with the rain, so could the Princess – and with her usual serenity she simply asked for her brolly and raincoat, and set off for an unhurried walkabout.

Apart from the hairstyle which became an instant craze when her engagement was announced, the Princess did for ruffled collars what the Queen Mother has done for pastel-shades.

The garlands were presented to the Royal couple on their trip round a stadium filled with 45,000 schoolchildren in Auckland, New Zealand. It was there the Princess first publicly 'hongied' or nose rubbed – a Maori form of greeting. Earlier on the tour an old Maori Princess had caught the Prince's attention and hongied with him. She made him promise to show his wife the art.

Unwittingly the Princess is the cause of many rifled jewellery boxes. When she hurtled into the fashion scene after her engagement many young ladies wanted to copy Lady Diana's successful style. They noted she often wore pretty, multi-stranded pearl chokers, so many a mother's jewellery box was turned inside out in a bid to find something similar. If all else failed there was soon a flood

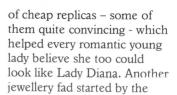

of cheap replicas – some of them quite convincing - which helped every romantic young lady believe she too could look like Lady Diana. Another jewellery fad started by the

Princess was the habit of wearing valuable pieces of jewellery – such as precious stone earrings – with ultra-casual clothes as if the jewellery was in fact fake.

On tour the Princess' wardrobe is of prime interest to many of the photographers and journalists on the Royal trail. A new outfit means that pictures of the Princess are more than usually likely to be published. And for the writers it means hours of telephone calls to try to find out who designed the dress, suit or coat. The Palace will not reveal the Princess' designers until she issues her warrants – possibly in 1984.

Barbara Daly did the bride's make-up for the wedding day, and one of the main features of her work was greenish foundation to take down Lady Diana Spencer's naturally high colour – and to reduce the effect of bridal blushes. But since then the Princess has rarely used a professional make-up artist, and she has never taken one on tour. As Barbara Daly herself remarked, the Princess is naturally so pretty her face needs little outside help.

Lady Diana Spencer's red Mini Metro, number plate MPB 909W (below) became bait for many eager newshounds. Where it went they followed – even when it was cleverly used by Lady Diana as a decoy. At and photographers who followed her almost constantly for months, and instead maintained a friendly but formal relationship with Fleet Street. Her flatmates Virginia Pitman, Carolyn Pride and Anne

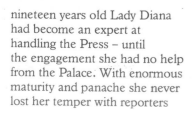

nineteen years old Lady Diana had become an expert at handling the Press – until the engagement she had no help from the Palace. With enormous maturity and panache she never lost her temper with reporters Bolton gave as much help as they could and firmly refused to make any revelations about the girl whose name was linked so closely to that of Prince Charles. Lady Diana's sisters also provided safe refuges when cat and mouse games with the Press got too hot. In the end 'Shy Di' was, and is, more than able to stand on her own two feet.

The whole world waited for The Kiss on the Palace balcony overlooking The Mall. Since their wedding day the Princess has brought a breath of fresh air to Prince Charles. Today the Royal couple, still clearly so in love, kiss, hold hands and share private jokes in public. The young Princess has helped bring out in the bachelor days on evenings off he sometimes dined alone – and when it came to his despatch boxes he attended to them alone or with some advice from a member of his household. On tour together the Royal couple have taken to sitting in the same room to do their work, and on their occasional evenings off Down

open Prince Charles' naturally loving and sensitive nature. She has also filled the lonely gap left for Prince Charles while he toured. In his

Under and in Canada they liked to dine together well away from the crowds, Press, entourage and all the pressures of touring.

Fairly small crowds turned out to see the Royal couple as they drove 100 miles or so across Tasmania, but crowds in the two major towns – Hobart and Launceston – made up for earlier disappointments. A week or so later in New Zealand a Royal-hungry world public got the pictures for which it had been waiting. Prince William of Wales held his first mass Press photo call (facing page). Dressed in traditional Royal baby wear – a smocked romper two piece with pearl buttons, and bare feet – William behaved beautifully. And he even played happily with the Buzzy

Bee toy, an institution in New Zealand, much to the delight of Prince Charles, who carried the toy from the Government House nursery to the rug spread on the lawn for Prince William and his parents.

Getting on and off the Royal launch, or aeroplanes, could be embarrassing for the Princess if she didn't have her wardrobe prepared. The dress and suit (below and far right) have slim skirts which cannot be caught by the wind. The Queen solves the problem be weighting some of her hems. Practical considerations are just as important to Royal wardrobes as colour and cut – for instance, the Princess' hem lines are long so she can bend to talk to children, or old people in wheelchairs.

On and off duty the Princess has a clever knack of combining various ensembles in such a way that she appears to be wearing 'new' clothes. (Below) she is wearing a quilted jacket with a Jan Vanvelden shirt designed to go with one of his silk suits. Here she is wearing it to a polo match when Prince Charles was playing for the Blue Devils. Later she wore the

same successful combination – down to the salmon pink shoes - to a trotting race in Canada. The Princess buys carefully and despite rumours that she spends thousands of pounds a week to keep her wardrobe up to scratch those who sell to her say she is very prudent – not that they, or Buckingham Palace, will say how much the Princess actually spends. As one designer put it: 'She chooses slowly and deliberately – unlike Jackie O for instance – who will buy every colour in a range of clothes is she finds a style she feels suits her.' Another strong trait in the Princess' fashion sense is her ability to find all kinds of different and unusual collars - its a good thing she does, for 'head

and shoulder' shots of her are very common, and they are made all the more interesting by varied collar styles. On this page the Princess is wearing a stand up collar under a ruffled collar, a neckerchief tied cowboy style, and on the facing page she is wearing a Puritan style collar, a floppy bow'd one and a more formal shirt collar. When she wears simple collars the Princess often adds a string or choker of pearls to show off her long neck.

Princess Grace of Monaco met Lady Diana Spencer at Goldsmiths Hall on the future Princess' first-ever formal engagement with Prince Charles. There was an instant rapport between the two women. When, the following year, Princess Grace died following a road accident just outside the little Principality of Monaco the Princess of Wales went to Monte Carlo to pay her last respects. Clearly distressed by the sudden death of her friend, the Princess of Wales was pictured bent with grief as she left the funeral to return to Balmoral. But despite her grief the Princess returned with the comforting knowledge that she had earned another feather for her Royal cap – she had completed her first solo engagement outside Britain with all the aplomb of an old campaigner.

Whatever the weather on tour in Australia, Canada or New Zealand, the Princess of Wales brought her own sunshine with her. Sometimes that seemed to be reflected in the warm yellow dresses and hats she wore.

Eyebrows were raised during a dinner on the Royal couple's visit to St John. Premier Hatfield made an eccentric speech and then told the Prince and Princess to stop as they left – because grace hadn't been said.

Prince William, the Press was told, would not make any appearances when the Royal couple flew from their home from home on the New South Wales' sheep station Woomargama to Melbourne for the last leg of their Australian tour. But those of us waiting for the Royal plane at Melbourne were in for a pleasant surprise. A sleepy looking Prince William in a natty blue and white romper suit was carried from the aircraft by Nanny Barnes and handed to his mother the Princess. A rosy cheeked Prince William was popped into the back seat of a waiting car, and strapped into a sheepskin-covered baby seat for the journey to Government House in Melbourne.

Hachi, the London-based Japanese designer who created the Princess' silk and crystal beaded one shouldered dress (right) insists his customers have good figures. 'I design dresses to show off a woman's body,' said Hachi, 'and I like a woman to look after her body so that she looks good in my clothes.' Thanks to regular exercise which includes almost daily swims, and a healthy diet, the super-trim Princess is an ideal customer.

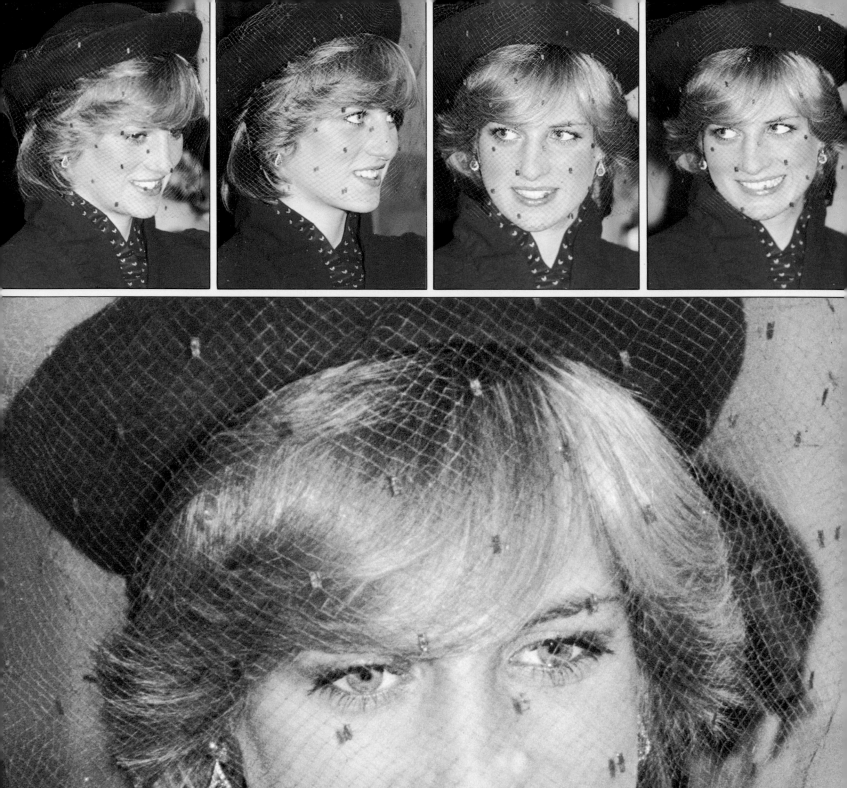

With over sixty years difference between them, the Queen Mother and the Princess have a lot in common. Both married for love and found themselves the focus of admiring world attention.

Romance is the key to both the Queen Mother, whose Castle of Mey is a setting for any self respecting fairy tale, and for the Princess whose wedding dress was fit for a fairytale Princess.

*Britannia* sailed into St John harbour for the Royal visit early on the morning of June 17th 1983. Tugs, boats and ships, hooted and fog-horned their welcome and in doing so woke many St John inhabitants and, no doubt, the Prince and Princess themselves. Royal

A vision of pale cream silk and snow white lacy flounces, diamonds and pearls, the Princess charmed Prime Minister Pierre Trudeau at the Halifax banquet he held in honour of the Royal couple at the beginning of their Canadian Tour.

Yacht officers were at a loss – noise is kept to a minimum when Royals are sleeping on board but there was no way anyone could stop the enthusiastic harbour welcome.

Every flower in the bride's bouquet was British grown – and the myrtle and veronica were taken from cuttings from Queen Victoria's bridal bouquet. At the centre of Prince Charles' bride's bouquet there were gardenias surrounded by white orchids, stephanotis, lily of the valley and white freesia.

Blue suits the Princess – it brings out the colour of her eyes. The warm blue coat pictured above was just what the Princess needed when she visited Upper Hutt and

Masterton, in New Zealand. Later the Royal couple flew to Wanganui to visit Prince Edward, who was spending the last few weeks of his two terms there as a master at Wanganui Collegiate. Prince Edward wore a Ngati Awa tribe feathered cloak, a very beautiful and highly prized piece of clothing...but somehow it didn't quite go with his suit.

Crowds in Brisbane (left) were so thick the Royal party and their police guard could hardly push through. One well-wisher placed a garland around the Princess' neck – others at the back of the crowd threw their flowers to her.

Wearing a shimmering red, flounce-necked evening dress, the Princess arrived for a State reception at Hobart looking less than happy with life (right). But when Prince Charles made one of his light-hearted speeches – gently teasing his Princess, her smile reappeared. No one knew the reason for her gloom – she had spent the morning on a successful walkabout, and the afternoon resting.

The Spencer tiara, although only on loan from the family collection, became an important part of the Princess' evening wardrobe Down Under. By the time she wore it for a State banquet in Wellington her regular hairdresser Kevin Shanley had returned to London to be replaced by Richard Dalton.

Among those closest to the Princess while she is working is her Lady-in-Waiting. On tour in Canada it was Anne Beckwith-Smith.

As the Royal newlyweds boarded Her Majesty's Yacht *Britannia* (left) they knew they could at last be alone for the second part of their honeymoon, after spending the first few days at the late Earl Mountbatten's home, Broadlands.

The Royal Yacht left Gibraltar in darkness. No other ship there could have kept pace or track. *Britannia*, it is said, can reach speeds of around 23 knots, and she carried her Royal love birds on their cruise in total secrecy.

In Edmonton the Princess wore a dramatic red and white suit and skirt (below) designed by Jan Vanvelden. But for once the Prince was getting as much attention as the Princess, and several girls on the walkabout route begged for permission to kiss him.

The Princess is rarely without flowers – wherever she goes her adoring public hands posies to her. When visiting London's Great Ormond Street Hospital a little boy announced, 'I ain't got no flowers for yer.' Cool as ever, the Princess replied, 'Never mind, smell these,' and waved a bouquet she had been given under the boy's nose. 'Yukk,' came the response.

Lady Diana's first Ascot with Prince Charles in 1981 (bottom centre) caused quite a stir. On one day during the week an official failed to recognise 'Lady Di' and refused to let her into the Royal enclosure because she wasn't wearing an enclosure badge. After a few seconds of astonished spluttering from nearby race-goers the embarrassed official realised his mistake. The Princess and her detective were then ushered into the enclosure.

The Princess is always in the pink...and sometimes she wears it too. Wearing the spotted Donald Campbell dress for the first time the Princess accomplished her first solo engagement on tour – a visit to Fremantle Hospital – and since then the Donald Campbell dress has become a great favourite. Her visit to the hospital went well, and on her way out of the wards she charmed the crowds by offering sympathy to the many sick people who were gathered there.

During the uproar of her engagement and newly wedded days the Princess used to rush into John Boyd's the hatter, in the Brompton Arcade, shouting, 'Don't worry, it's only me'. 'Only me' fast became one of John Boyd's most important customers after

Princess Anne and Margaret Thatcher. But the Princess wasn't used to wearing hats, and sometimes wore them back to front and even sideways. Many said the hats looked better for it – either way the Princess' hats sparked off a hat revival.

The Princess first wore the traditional square necked green ball gown for official engagement pictures. Later she wore it to a gala of Welsh music and dance in Swansea. The once filled-to-brimming dress was beginning to hang off the Princess. The following month, on November 5th 1981, Buckingham Palace announced that the Princess was expecting her first baby.

Her sudden slimness was partly explained – the Princess was suffering from morning sickness.

On the facing page the main picture shows the Princess walking with her hands clenched – she developed the habit to cover her bitten finger nails. Her clenched fists are not a sign of frustrated anger!

Soon after Prince William was born the Princess wore the pearl and gold necklace with a heart shaped pendant for the first time. As a result many newspapers announced that it was a 'baby present' from Prince Charles. In fact it is thought to be a present from the Princess' own family. By Royal standards the Princess does not yet have a large collection of jewellery. On the facing page she is wearing, in addition to the necklace, the Queen Mary diamond and pearl tiara with matching earrings borrowed from the Queen and (left) she is wearing the same drop earrings teamed with a string of pearls, Those pearls are seen again in the bottom picture.

On the opposite page the Princess' necklace glitters with the Prince of Wales feathers. Somewhere in the Princess' jewel collection there is another Prince of Wales feathers necklace, this one set with sapphires.

One of the suits Lady Diana Spencer wore to Ascot (above) with Prince Charles a few weeks before their wedding she later wore to a small town church service in Holbrook, New South Wales. Made by David Neill, it is a three piece silk suit.

David Neill made another Royal hit with this red silk dress patterned with stars of yellow, blue and green (bottom

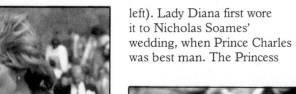

left). Lady Diana first wore it to Nicholas Soames' wedding, when Prince Charles was best man. The Princess

next wore it on the final day of the Australian tour with a large, blue, digger-style hat, in honour of the host country.

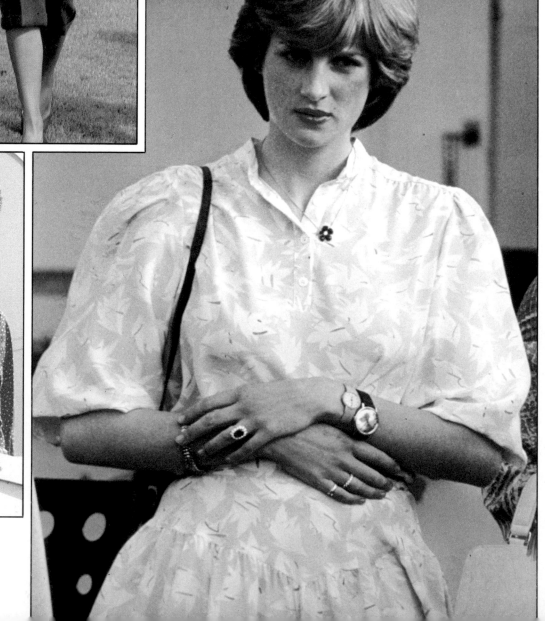

From her engagement days, the Princess wore Prince Charles' wristwatch while he played polo.

Riding through the bush in Victoria, a couple of men on horseback spotted the Prince and Princess of Wales on the platform at the back of the train travelling from

Melbourne to Ballarat. The riders spurred on their horses and chased the train, whooping and cheering their greeting to the Royal couple. They gave the morning a zany, Wild West atmosphere. Later that day the Prince and Princess visited a working reconstruction of an 1830s gold rush town.

The first time Lady Diana Spencer came across designs by Emanuel, makers of That Dress (centre bottom) was the moment she spotted one of their pale pink bow and ruffle blouses at a Snowdon photo session. Lady Diana had agreed to the session for a Vogue personality sitting in November 1980 – the blouse was among the clothes chosen by Vogue. She liked it so much she wore it for the Snowdon pictures and later got in

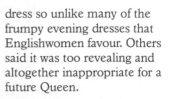

dress so unlike many of the frumpy evening dresses that Englishwomen favour. Others said it was too revealing and altogether inappropriate for a future Queen.

touch with the Emanuels to find a suitable evening dress for her first formal engagement with Prince Charles. At their workshop she settled for a low cut strapless ballgown decorated with ruffles and sequins. When the Princess-to-be saw it, it was in shell form but it was soon completed for her to wear to Goldsmiths Hall. Public and

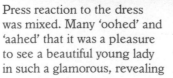

Press reaction to the dress was mixed. Many 'oohed' and 'aahed' that it was a pleasure to see a beautiful young lady in such a glamorous, revealing

Floods had subsided by the time the Royal Party's Royal Australian Air Force Boeing 707 touched down at Alice Springs (facing page) for the start of their six week Australian Tour. Torrential rain in the previous week meant the Royal couple had to stay at the newly-opened Gap

bedroom she later scolded him, 'You must not do that. It's very naughty. I saw you.' she said half serious, half teasing, as she wagged her finger at the man she thought to be the culprit. The photographer indignantly denied any bad behaviour. The Princess, unconvinced,

Motor Lodge instead of the then-flooded Federal Hotel as originally planned. No sooner had the Prince and Princess settled in than they were under siege from an enthusiastic crowd of Press and public The Princess of Wales was not amused, and when she spotted one photographer apparently pointing a camera in the direction of her continued to scold her victim. But by and large the Princess has a good relationship with Fleet St as does The Prince of Wales.

It was at Banbury, (facing page) in Australia, that the Prince swore when his speech notes blew away. To make matters worse he had just explained to the assembled thirteen thousand schoolchildren the importance of decorum and seemly behaviour! The Princess managed to stifle a giggle. Things got off to a bad start that day when rain delayed the Royal arrival by over half an hour. But nothing could dampen the Royal couple's good spirits. The Princess, in a demure grey silk Caroline Charles jacket and skirt, with sailor collared white blouse, held hands with the Prince as they drove from the stadium to a civic reception.

In St John and the seaboard tour stops in Canada the couple used *Britannia* to entertain their hosts.

Celebrations began on the last night of the Canadian Tour (right) in honour of the Princess' birthday the following day. But she had already received one of her most unusual birthday presents from the Captain of *HMCS Assiniboine*, *Britannia's* naval escort. Commander Moore, hearing about the Princess' interest in the icebergs outside St John's harbour, had despatched a small

boatload of his men to chip a 30lb piece of iceberg for her Royal Highness. The mini iceberg was popped into a pale blue coolbox and presented to the Princess in St John's. She was delighted with it.

Wearing a tartan wool dress and typical ruffled collar, the Princess planted a tree in Hyde Park to commemorate her wedding year. Prince Charles gave her a hand at one point, but the Princess, as independent as ever, completed the planting single-handed. (Below left) the Princess made a variation to her red maternity coat by arranging this silk and lace collar and black velvet tie over it.

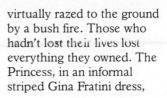

There was another, less light-hearted, tree planting for the Princess when she visited the tragedy-torn town of Cockatoo in Victoria (bottom centre). Weeks before it had been

virtually razed to the ground by a bush fire. Those who hadn't lost their lives lost everything they owned. The Princess, in an informal striped Gina Fratini dress,

apologised over and over again for bothering inhabitants at such a time – but her presence and concern gave the people the impetus to make a new start.

A Civil and Public Services Association picket was waiting for the Princess when she made a solo visit to the Department of Health and Social Security Headquarters at the Elephant and Castle, wearing a brown tweed wrapover coat (facing page). It could have been an awkward situation for the young Princess, but, dignified as ever, she concentrated so hard on smiling at the crowd that she never caught the eyes of the pickets. Later the Princess lunched at a restaurant, the *Menage a Trois* in Beauchamp Place, which had been given a security vetting the previous day. At the restaurant, which specialises

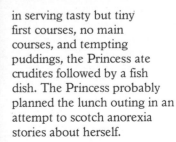

in serving tasty but tiny first courses, no main courses, and tempting puddings, the Princess ate crudites followed by a fish dish. The Princess probably planned the lunch outing in an attempt to scotch anorexia stories about herself.

Staff take care of the Princess' day-to-day domestic life, and so it must have made an interesting change for her to visit the International

Spring Fair at Birmingham National Exhibition Centre, which has one of the largest displays of consumer goods in Europe. In her bachelor girl days Lady Diana was, by all accounts, very domesticated and earned the nickmane of 'Tidy Di' because she was said to clear up after her flatmates in Coleherne Court, Chelsea. She also did a

comprehensive, though exclusive, course at a Wimbledon cookery school – and so she can turn out everything from a traditional English steak and kidney pudding to some of the more exotic *cordon bleu* dishes. And now, of course, she has become an expert on baby care, and likes to involve herself with her son's day to day welfare.

Prince Charles' silver Welsh dragon mascot is just visible through the windscreen of his DB6 Aston Martin (below). He also has a polo player mascot which is fixed to his Ford Granada. For her twenty-first birthday the Prince gave the Princess a silver frog mascot for her Ford Escort in honour of his married nickmane 'the frog prince'. The mascot tradition was begun by the Queen, who has an Edward Seago St George and the Dragon attached to whichever State car she is using. Like all the Royal family the Princess uses her personal car when she wants to drive around London or the countryside unnoticed. Unfortunately the Princess sparked off a row in the winter of 1982-1983 when her car was found parked on double yellow lines in London.

No wonder the Princess of Wales has earned a reputation as one of Britain's best advertisements for fashion. Apart from her charm and good looks her legs seem to go on forever. The pale blue and white candy-striped trousers topped by a blouse she normally wears with a Caroline Charles suit helped the Princess keep cool and look chic at a polo match. Later she and the Prince looked at some polo equipment to give this unusual Royal pose (top right).

Anne Beckwith-Smith, the Lady-in-Waiting most frequently seen with the Princess of Wales, is seen bottom centre. Her royal work – which has no salary – is no easy task. Behind the scenes she has to help with the Princess' correspondence and organise diary dates. On duty she has to be on hand to cope with disasters such as laddered tights or a broken zip, and she has to help carry flowers given to the Princess on walkabouts.

Sinclair Hill, pictured on the facing page chatting to the Prince and Princess, is the Prince's polo mentor and friend. When the Prince visited Sinclair Hill's native country, Australia, in his pre-marriage days he once stayed on the Hill's family property. On tour in Australia the Prince and Princess met Sinclair at a Warwick Farm polo match, and more recently the threesome met up again in England. While the Prince is playing polo the Princess

still has one of her detectives for company. On polo afternoons the Princess is not on parade and she wears casual clothes, but gone is the time soon after her engagement when she wore ultra-casual dungarees.

The Princess, dressed in her going away outfit, (recently altered to give the jacket long sleeves) is seen here 'working the crowds' with her usual good humour. With a firm handshake and a few well chosen words for as many of the crowd as possible in the time allocated, the Princess of Wales makes her work look easy. But she had to learn her

new job under the spotlight of world publicity. It was enough to make an old campaigner nervous – but the Princess never baulked. To begin with, her enthusiasm meant she took longer over her walkabouts and visits than her advisors planned, but after three weeks on tour Down Under her timing was near perfect.

Lady Sarah Armstrong-Jones (right, top right and facing page) stood in for the Princess while her father, Lord Snowdon, organised lighting for a sitting with baby Prince William and his parents. Holding a doll wrapped in a shawl Lady Sarah posed as the Princess.

Parker-Bowles, made their homes available for weekends. Balmoral was not such a good bet – it is well known to the Press who can normally find out who is staying there as whose guest.

Prince Charles' and Lady Diana's courtship was not an easy one. The Press decided early on in the proceedings that Earl Spencer's daughter was the future Princess of Wales. And they followed her every footstep. But their respective families were on hand to help. The Queen Mother lent her Scottish Castle, Birkhall, near Balmoral, for a weekend. The Prince's friends, too, notably the Tryons and

Benny Ong's cool, crepe-de-chine peppermint skirt and ivory top was first worn for the Princess' visit to Tennant Creek in the Australian outback – it was just the thing for the scorching desert heat.

Jan Vanvelden's drop waisted turquoise silk sailor suit stole the show on a night-time engagement in London. The Princess' slim hips are shown off by the low waist style.

Her chic has rubbed off on Prince Charles, and since his marriage the only suits he has had made are three elegant, double breasted ones, a far cry from his old-fashioned single breasted suits.

Earl Spencer (below) dotes on his daughter the Princess. I visited him at his stately home, Althorp, soon after Lady Diana's engagement to the Prince was announced. 'It's not easy being number three in the family as Diana is, you know,' he said. 'It's neither one thing nor the other – she has always been such a sweet girl.' As he spoke about his daughter his voice swelled with pride – he could hardly express his delight about her engagement. And the Princess' mother, the Hon Mrs Shand Kydd, has been a staunch ally, especially when times were rough. When Press attention became too much for her daughter Mrs Shand Kydd wrote to The Times to complain.

It was almost two years to the
day since they were married
when the Prince and Princess
took a trip down memory lane
and passed St Paul's Cathedral
on their way to a lunch date
at London's Guildhall (these
pages).

# Diana's Fashion Diary

1981

**February 25**   Press Photo call after the official announcement of her engagement to the Prince of Wales.   *Delphinium-blue two-piece suit with long reverse-pleated skirt, and buttonless jacket gathered at the waist under an integral bow. Deep open neck showing a white silk blouse with blue seagull motifs, high neck and with large bow at the lefthand side. Black shoes.*

**March 3**   Attended the première of the film *For Your Eyes Only*, West End, London.   *Full length evening dress in flame-red with glittering gold spot pattern. Low, shaped neckline with thin shoulder straps. Gold and cornelian necklace. Silver accessories.*

**March 9**   Attended a recital of music at Goldsmiths Hall, London.   *Strapless low-cut black taffeta evening dress with full skirt. Matching taffeta shawl with ornate ruffled edges. Silver necklace with small pendant and matching earrings. Black evening bag and matching shoes.*

**March 25**   Visited Sandown Park Races.   *Brown two-piece outfit with midi-length skirt and loose, open jacket over a white blouse with a high frill neck. Matching brown trilby hat, and brown accessories.*

**March 27**   Visited Gloucestershire Police Constabulary Headquarters, Cheltenham.   *Deep-blue two-piece suit with long jacket gathered at the waist and deep white sailor collars meeting under a red ribbon bow at the front. Pearl collar and matching earrings.*

**April**   Official photograph taken at Highgrove House for use in Royal Wedding Souvenir Booklet.   *Bright apple-green silk taffeta evening dress with short puffed sleeves, low, round neck and a full skirt. Heavy earrings of hanging diamonds, and diamond necklace.*

**May 9**   Attended the opening of the Mountbatten exhibition, Broadlands, Romsey, Hampshire.   *Bright green two-piece suit with front-pleated skirt and pleated jacket with line of buttons running down the centre. Sleeves, sash and skirt hem bordered or highlighted with wide bands of blue, green and mauve. White silk blouse with double ruff at the neck. Black shoes and a clutch bag.*

**May 14**   Attended the presentation by the Queen of new colours to the Welsh Guards at Windsor Castle.   *White silk dress with tiny regular L-shaped motifs in grey and maroon, and trimmed and edged with golden-yellow silk. Long full sleeves with buttoned yellow cuffs; panelled yoke and a row of yellow buttons from neck to waist. Matching yellow ribbons at neck. Primrose-coloured hat with up-turned brim and matching ostrich feathers flecked with brown. White shoes.*

**May 22**   Visited General Hospital, Tetbury.

**May 22**   Attended a Thanksgiving service at St Mary's Church, Tetbury.   *Two-piece flame-coloured outfit consisting of a plain skirt and a silk, deep V-necked jacket with a snow storm white pattern. Underneath, a white blouse with frilled, stand-up collar. Black self-patterned bag and matching shoes.*

**May 27**   Attended a Welsh Guards dinner-dance at Merchant Taylors' Hall, London.   *Full-length evening dress in bright red with all-over gold spot pattern and a shaped, frilled neckline held with thin straps. Three row pearl choker, and silver accessories.*

**June 1**   Attended the wedding of Nicholas Soames and Catherine Weatherall at St Margaret's, Westminster.   *Bright red silk dress patterned with tiny white stars and larger stars in blue and green. Matching belt and pie-frill neck and cuffs. Matching red hat with broad silk band and wide flyaway brim ornamented with a huge bow at the back. Red handbag and matching shoes.*

**June 11**   Attended a State Banquet given by King Khalid of Saudi Arabia at Claridges Hotel, London.   *Pale smoke-grey chiffon ball dress with silver spot diamante pattern. Overlaid bodice providing deep flouncing at the neck and waist and see-through sleeves. Pale pink silk bow at the centre of deep V-neck and broad matching sash. Long white gloves. Diamond necklace and earrings. Silver evening bag and shoes.*

**June 13**   Attended the Queen's Birthday Parade, Horseguards Parade.   *Two-piece suit, predominantly sky-blue with small abstract design in white and pink. Loose open jacket with long full sleeves, over a white silk blouse with large frilled collar overlaying the neck of the jacket. Deep-pink waist sash at the top of the skirt. Matching blue-veiled pillbox hat worn over the right temple with a huge white flower at the front. Three row pearl choker. White accessories.*

**June 15**   Attended the Service of the Order of the Garter, St George's Chapel, Windsor Castle.   *Light-green two-piece silk suit with front-pleated skirt and pleated jacket with a line of blue buttons running down the centre. Sleeves, sash and skirt hem bordered or highlighted with wide bands of blue, green and mauve. Wide-brimmed green hat with narrow blue band. Black accessories.*

June 16          Attended the first day of Royal Ascot.          *Striped dress in mauve, grey and white with low straight neckline underneath a matching jacket with pleat-frilled collar and cuffs. Matching mauve picture hat with splay-feathered trimming over the brim. White gloves and shoes.*

June 17          Attended second day of Royal Ascot.          *Peach-coloured silk suit with fold-over jacket over a white silk blouse with wide flounced overlaying collar. Narrow white tie-belt over the jacket. White hat with pink gardenia on the right side. Choker consisting of three strings of pearls. White accessories.*

June 18          Attended the third day of Royal Ascot.          *Red and white candy-striped blouse with large collars, central bow, and full sleeves. Loose, sleeveless academic-style overgarment in tomato red, matching a straight skirt. Red straw hat with white flowers at the back, and matching red handbag and shoes. Choker of three strings of pearls.*

June 19          Attended the last day of Royal Ascot.          *Pale blue and white squared dress with narrow white collars, two parallel rows of blue buttons running from neck to waist, and matching blue-buckled sash. Edwardian-style bonnet in white with veiling tied under the chin. White accessories.*

July 3          Attended the finals of the men's tennis championship at Wimbledon.          *Flower-patterned two-piece outfit in red, white, yellow and pink, on a bright blue background. Jacket with three-quarter length sleeves and a tie-belt at the waist. Underneath, a white silk blouse with V-neck, small collars and tight cuffs. Single row of pearls and white accessories.*

July 15          Attended an exhibition at the Royal Academy of Arts, London.          *Midnight-blue evening dress with regular pattern of silver sequins. Close-fitting bodice with low neck, and slender silver straps.*

July 24          Visited the Army Barracks at Tidworth, Hampshire.          *White silk dress with tiny regular L-shaped motifs in grey and maroon, trimmed and edged with golden-yellow silk. Long full sleeves with buttoned, yellow cuffs; panelled yoke, and a row of yellow buttons from neck to waist. Matching yellow ribbons at the neck. White shoes and clutch bag.*

July 29          Marriage to the Prince of Wales at St Paul's Cathedral, London.          *Ivory-coloured dress in silk taffeta with puff-ball skirt, the shaped bodice of silk taffeta encrusted with sequins and mother of pearl, and with intricately-embroidered lace panels to front and back. Low V-shaped neckline bearing a ruffle of taffeta overlaid with pearl-encrusted lace, and a huge Victorian bow at the centre. Puffed sleeves pointed at the shoulders and gathered at the elbows. Hand embroidered gossamer silk veil, sweeping train of diaphanous silk trimmed with embroidered lace. Soft ivory-coloured silk slipper shoes, top-stitched with an Elizabethan lattice design, with a mother of pearl sequin in each section and a heart-shaped, lace-frilled motif at the tongue. Finely fluted heels hand-painted in gold. Spencer family tiara of entwined heart and flower design, and heavy drop earrings.*

July 29          Departure from Buckingham Palace to begin honeymoon at Broadlands.          *Pale-cantaloupe silk tussore dress with cummerbund sash at the waist and small slit at the hem on the left hand side. Short-sleeved bolero jacket in matching fabric, with frilled white silk organza collars joined by a large bow, and with organza trim on the sleeves. Small straw tricorn hat in matching pink, veiled and trimmed with ostrich feather. Victorian-style choker of six rows of pearls, and small pearl earrings. Pink shoes and matching silk pochette-style handbag.*

August 1          Departure from Romsey via Gibraltar for honeymoon on board the *Royal Yacht Britannia*.          *Long white silk two-piece outfit with elegant flower-spray motifs in red, blue and green, the jacket loose-fitting and self-tying at the midriff. Underneath, a mid-blue vest edged in white. Three string pearl choker. White accessories.*

August 12          Met President and Madame Sadat, Cairo, Egypt.          *Shell-pink silk dress with long sleeves, low V-neck and matching tie belt. Coral-pink necklace. White accessories.*

August 13          Entertained President and Madame Sadat on board the *Royal Yacht Britannia* at Port Said, Egypt.          *Long black taffeta evening gown with horizontal gold and silver stripes on the bodice, and wider bands on the skirt. Low horizontal neckline, and ribbon straps over the shoulder. Informal tie-belt waistband. Small pearl earrings.*

August 19          Photo call for the Press and journalists at the Brig o' Dee, Balmoral.          *Casual two-piece outfit in brown, dull-blue and white dog-tooth pattern. White, collared blouse beneath an open jacket, with brown leather buttons down the centre. White shoes.*

September 4          Attended the Braemar Games, Aberdeenshire.          *Red and black plaid dress-coat with flared skirt and padded full sleeves. Broad, stand-up collar with a row of small black buttons running down to a waistband tied with a knotted black belt. Black tam-o'-shanter hat, and black accessories.*

October 27          Visited towns in North Wales.          *Two-piece suit consisting of a bottle-green dress, slightly flared, beneath a close fitting blood-red jacket. The jacket cut to reveal the dress's frilled cuffs and tie bow at the neck. Matching red hat with flyaway brim and large red bow at the back. Red shoes and handbag.*

October 28          Visited towns in West and mid-Wales.          *Warm blond-brown cashmere coat, loose-fitting and long-lapelled, with a tie belt. Blouse of white silk with frill at the neck. Soft, matching saucer hat with large ostrich feather on right hand side. Brown accessories.*

October 28          Attended a gala concert at Brangwen Hall Swansea.          *Emerald-green taffeta evening dress with deep square neck and short sleeves, beneath a copious black velvet cape. Diamond and emerald choker with matching earrings. Silver evening bag and shoes.*

**October 29**    Visited towns in South Wales.    *Two-piece suit in aubergine velvet; a generously flared skirt and close-fitting jacket with front button panel enclosed by pale white piping. The heavily-frilled collar of a white silk blouse visible above the neck. Small, matching, aubergine, brimmed hat with cascade of ostrich feather falling on the right hand side. Black shoes and clutch bag.*

**October 29**    Received the Freedom of the City of Cardiff at City Hall, Cardiff.    *Wedgewood-blue silk chiffon cocktail dress with mustard and white leaf pattern. Ruched bodice and high-frilled neckline. Sapphire and diamond earrings. Blue accessories.*

**November 2**    Visited the National Film Theatre, South Bank, London, for the opening of the 25th London Film Festival.    *Green-black midi-length velvet dress with large white lace collar overlaid at the yoke. Narrow lace trim to the hem of dress. Matching green satin shoes.*

**November 2**    Attended the State Opening of Parliament, Palace of Westminster.    *Full-length formal dress in ivory-silk embroidered with occasional large flower-spray design. Deep V-neck and full, sequin-embroidered elbow-length sleeves. Long white gloves. Pearl drop tiara and a three row pearl choker.*

**November 4**    Attended the opening of the exhibition "Splendours of the Gonzaga", Victoria and Albert Museum, London.    *Light, filmy, off-the-shoulder evening dress of silk chiffon. Predominantly white with soft, swirling designs in pink and blue, with sequined diagonals across the whole garment. The neckline generously frilled and topped by pale blue bows matching the broad waistband. Choker consisting of six rows of pearls, and silver accessories.*

**November 5**    Attended a luncheon given by the Lord Mayor of London, Guildhall, London.    *Thick, flame-red coat woven in Welsh wool, striped stitch-effect with vertical lines of blue and yellow. Heavy fringing at collar, cuffs and hem. Underneath, a waistcoat in similar material, over a blue blouse frilled at the neck and cuffs. Small mid-blue wool hat, veiled and feathered. Matching shoes and handbag.*

**November 7**    Attended the Royal British Legion Festival of Remembrance, Royal Albert Hall, London.    *Simple, black silk dress with subtle grey spots. Round, medium-level neckline, and spray of poppies on left hand side. Simple string of pearls, and black accessories.*

**November 8**    Attended the Remembrance Day Service, Cenotaph, Whitehall.    *Black coat-dress with a white silk lace-edged yoke bearing a black bow at the centre. Black feathered hat, and black accessories.*

**November 12**    Visited York and Chesterfield.    *Silk dress patterned with regular abstract designs in black, red and white. White frilled collars and cuffs, and a black bow at the centre of the neck. Tall-crowned black hat with black gloves, shoes and handbag.*

**November 18**    Switched on the Christmas lights, Regent Street, London.    *Black satin two-piece suit over a white blouse with cravat-style neck. Piping on the back collar of the suit, brought forward as loose tassels in the front. Silver shoes and black watered-silk clutch bag.*

**November 19**    Planted three cherry trees in The Copse, Hyde Park, London.    *Red and black plaid dress-coat with flared skirt and padded, full sleeves. Broad stand-up collar with row of small black buttons running down to a waistband tied with a knotted black belt. Ruffle of a white silk blouse visible at the neck. Brown shoes.*

**November 23**    Opened the new Post Office, Northampton.    *Bottle-green two-piece suit with a jacket heavily embroidered on the front seams with flower patterns in red, pink, white and cream. Pale pink blouse with large frilled collar overlaying the jacket. Loose, turban-style hat in matching green with large feather feature. Bottle-green accessories. Three rows of pearls worn as a choker.*

**November 30**    Visited the Royal Opera House Covent Garden to see a performance of Romeo and Juliet.    *Long black evening dress with warm, hip-length jacket in white fur. Single row of pearls. Black accessories.*

**December 10**    Attended a Christmas Carol Service, Gloucester Cathedral.    *Grey tailored cossack-style coat with high stand-up collars. Matching astrakhan hat with bow at the side, complemented by a large matching muff. Black knee-length boots.*

**December 21**    Attended a Christmas Celebration at Guildford Cathedral.    *Bright-red wool coat over a matching red skirt, and blouse of matching colour with small green and white butterfly design. Matching red hat with upturned brim and full-face veiling. Red shoes, black gloves and clutch bag.*

**December 25**    Attended the Christmas Morning Service at St George's Chapel, Windsor.    *Below-the-knee coat in turquoise wool, with leaf-green embroidered panels and pockets, and pink, plum and gold flower designs on the yoke and pockets. Small matching turquoise pillbox hat. Aquamarine handbag and shoes. Black gloves.*

## 1982

**January 23**    Visited the January Fair at the Dick Sheppard School, Tulse Hill, London.    *Outfit as worn at St George's Chapel Windsor (above) but without hat or gloves.*

**February 2**    Attended the British Film Institute Dinner, 11 Downing Street, London.    *Deep-sapphire evening dress, lavishly trimmed with white lace fichu and corresponding lace ruffles at the cuffs. Low-cut plunging neckline. Diamond drop earrings with sapphire centres. Pearl necklace with sapphire centre. Silver clutch bag and shoes.*

February 11    Visited the studios of Independent Television, London.    *Loose shift dress with three-quarter length sleeves, over long, full sleeved, ruff-necked, white blouse. Wide, generous, white collar, overlaying the yoke of the dress, with a dark bow and falling ribbons at the centre of the neck. Soft slipper shoes, with large bows.*

February 16    Left London for ten-day holiday in the Bahamas.    *Pale-cream shift dress beneath a warm white wool jacket. White shoes.*

February 27    Returned to London from the Bahamas.    *High-waisted maternity smock in blue and white gingham, with open neck showing the frill of a white blouse underneath. White woollen jacket, and white shoes.*

February 28    Attended a reception to mark the centenary of the Royal College of Music, St James's Palace.

February 28    Attended a service of Thanksgiving for the College, Westminster Abbey.    *Fuchsia-pink coat with wide apron-style panels at the yoke, a stand-up ruff at the neckline, and wide piping around the collar falling loose to the front with pom-poms. Matching hat with bow on the left underside of the wide brim. Black accessories.*

March 4    Attended a Gala Concert, Barbican Centre, London.    *Full-length silk burgundy dress in Jacobean style with deep square neckline bordered by a small cream frill, and white lace flounced beneath the three-quarter length flounced dress sleeves. Sun-ray diamond necklace, and diamond and pearl drop earrings. Silver evening bag and shoes.*

March 8    Attended the Charity Première of *The Little Foxes* at the Victoria Palace Theatre, London.    *Full-length champagne-coloured evening gown embroidered with sprays of sequins against a faintly squared background. Low-cut neckline complemented with ornate diamond necklace. Sleeves puffed and gathered. Silver evening bag and shoes.*

March 14    Attended a concert of music at the Royal Albert Hall.    *Tomato-red evening gown, maternity-style, with flashes of gold sequins crossing in diagonal formation. Narrow white trim at the low neck and cuffs. Single row of pearls. Voluminous black cape over the top for outdoor use.*

March 18    Visited the Cheltenham Horse Racing Festival on Gold Cup Day.    *Black maternity dress with white polka dots, ruffled at neck and sleeves, beneath a large loose mohair coat in red, with large collars laid over the shoulders. Matching red saucer hat with wide brim, and a large rosette at the back. Brown shoulder bag and shoes.*

March 22    Visited projects assisted by the Prince's Trust at Huddersfield and Newcastle upon Tyne.    *Black maternity dress with white polka dots, frilled at the collar and cuffs. Deep-pink coat in mohair with enormous fringed collars covering the shoulders and much of the bodice. Black clutch bag and shoes.*

March 30    Visited Roundhay Park, Leeds.

March 30    Opened St Gemma's Hospice, Leeds.    *Baize-green wool coat with large black Victorian Gothic motifs forming a continuous design from the front of the bodice to around the neck. Black trim on the cuffs and stand-up collars. Matching green hat, high-crowned, with a broad green silk band, and a bow and falling feathers on the right hand side. Black accessories.*

April 2    Attended the opening of the Chinese Community Centre, Liverpool.    *Fuchsia-pink coat with wide apron-style panels at the yoke, stand-up ruffles at the neckline, and wide piping around the collar, falling loose to the front with pom-poms. Matching hat with bow on the left underside of a wide brim. Black accessories.*

April 3    Attended the Grand National, Aintree.    *China-blue maternity dress with double ruffle down the bodice and an additional ruffle at the neck. A generous burgundy-red mohair coat with large collars laid over the shoulders. Matching red-felt saucer hat with wide brim and a rosette at the rear.*

April 7    Opened the new Sony Television Factory, Bridgend.    *Pastel-blue maternity dress patterned with white polka dots, and with long, frilled sleeves. Warm, pink, woollen military-style coat, toggled on the left hand side, and with tall stand-up collars. Three row pearl choker worn clasp to front. Small, pink pillbox hat with large satin rosette at the back. Pink clutch bag and matching shoes.*

April 20    Arrived in St Mary's, Scilly Isles.    *Simple green summer dress, sailor-style with white collars. White shoes.*

April 20    Toured St Mary's during an evening walkabout.    *White polka dot blue maternity dress with stand-up frills on the cuffs and flatter frills around the neckline. Single row of pearls. Black slipper shoes with bows.*

April 21    Visited the island of Tresco.    *Black dress with white polka dots, over a pink blouse with ribbons at the neck. A long black wool coat. Black shoes.*

April 22    Attended lunch for staff and tenants of the Duchy of Cornwall, St Mary's, Isle of Scilly.    *Flowing, self-patterned maternity dress in mid-blue, with open neck bordered by ruffles and revealing a pink blouse with tie neck beneath. Black handbag and black shoes.*

May 18    Opened the Albany Trust Community Centre, Deptford, London.    *White polka dot blue maternity dress with stand-up frills on the cuffs, and flatter frills below the neckline. Three row pearl choker. Black accessories.*

June 12       Attended the Trooping the Colour, Horseguards Parade.       *Emerald-green coat-dress, maternity-style, with half-length gathered sleeves, a gathered yoke line and V-neck wing collars. Small edged saucer hat with veiling and bow at the side. Three row pearl choker.*

June 17.       Attended Royal Ascot followed by polo on Smith's Lawn, Windsor.       *Long pale-pink maternity dress with round neck and long sleeves. The matching pink hat which was worn for Ascot was removed for the visit to Smith's Lawn, when the Princess wore a warm white wool cardigan. White accessories.*

June 22       Left St Mary's Hospital, Paddington after the birth of Prince William.       *Long green maternity dress with small white polka dots and white collars. Pink shoes.*

July 26       Attended the service of Thanksgiving and Reconciliation after the Falklands conflict, St Paul's Cathedral, London.       *Royal blue dress patterned with small black dots, buttoned to the left side of the neck and gathered at the waist by a broad tasselled black belt. The hem ornamented with large black Paisley motifs between patterned bands. Black straw veiled hat with small burst of matching feathers. Black accessories.*

August 4       Christening of Prince William, Buckingham Palace.       *Salmon-pink short-sleeved dress with close flower design in white and blue. Bodice gathered by matching belt tied in large bow at the side. Wide-brimmed straw hat in matching pink with silk band and bow. String of pearls bearing a heart-shaped pendant in the middle.*

September 3       Attended the wedding of Carolyn Pride, Chelsea Old Church, London.       *Raspberry pink, loose fitting silk dress with high neck, dropped waist, elbow length sleeves, and large white sailor collars. White straw platter hat with navy trim and matching petal bow beneath the brim. Three strand pearl choker, white quilted clutch bag and white shoes.*

September 4       Attended the Braemar Gathering, Aberdeenshire.       *Dull green and gold plaid effect squared dress, with stark white Peter Pan-style collars and cuffs. Perky Glengarry bonnet in bottle green velvet, with emerald trim and black ribbons. Black shoes and handbag.*

September 19       Attended the funeral of Princess Grace of Monaco, Monte Carlo.       *Black dress and coat with mandarin collar, broken only by a silver necklace with a heart-shaped locket. Wide-brimmed Spanish style straw hat with fully enveloping veil. Matching accessories.*

October 12       Paid an informal visit to London to accompany Prince Charles on his way to Portsmouth.       *White silk-satin Puritan blouse with lace trim and large black bow at the neck. Long wool cardigan and moire skirt.*

October 26       Attended a concert given by Mstislav Rostropovitch at the Barbican Centre, London.       *Emerald green silk taffeta full length evening dress, with square neck, short puffed sleeves and a matching silk waist band. Diamond and emerald choker and matching earrings; silver evening bag and shoes.*

October 29       Attended a performance by the Welsh National Opera, New Theatre, Cardiff.       *Pale blue-grey silk chiffon evening dress with sequin spots. Deep V-neck, and the bodice overlaid with a fine flounce to include see-through sleeves. Pale pink bow at décolletage, and matching broad sash. Heart-shaped pendant on a silver chain, and matching silver accessories.*

November 2       Opened a new extension to the Royal School for the Blind, Leatherhead, Surrey.       *Rich, deep-green velvet coat with close-fitting bodice buttoned down the centre, and voluminous skirt. Visible frills of the collar and cuffs of a white silk blouse. Small bowler-style hat in matching green velvet with a silk band and large bow at the back. Brown accessories.*

November 3       Attended the State Opening of Parliament, Palace of Westminster.       *Full length white chiffon dress beneath a pure white mink jacket. Spencer tiara and diamond splay necklace with pearl drop earrings.*

November 3       Attended a celebration tea in aid of the Pre-School Playgroup Association, Hyde Park Hotel, London.       *Mid-blue cocktail dress covered with a leaf design in gold and white. Full see-through sleeves gathered and frilled at three-quarter length; frills at the neckline above a ruched yoke. Matching clutch bag and court shoes.*

November 9       Attended a charity dinner and fashion show in aid of Birthright, Guildhall, London.       *Slender crepe-de-chine ankle-length silk dress with one shoulder neckline. Overall pattern of blue and white hoops on a rich mid-blue background. Double frill at the neck: at the dropped waistline a blue sash tied posy-effect at the side. Pearl drop earrings and three row pearl choker. Silver evening bag and shoes.*

November 10       Attended the opening of the Victorian Heyday Exhibition, Portsmouth.

November 10       Inspected the *Mary Rose*, Southsea.       *Grey wool coat-dress with slightly flared skirt, the bodice relieved by five pairs of black buttons down the centre and black collar and cuffs. Cherry red leather boots.*

November 10       Attended a dinner aboard *HMS Victory*, Portsmouth.       *Full length silk cerise dress in Jacobean style with deep square neckline bordered by a small cream frill and white lace flounced beneath the three-quarter length dress sleeves. Single row of pearls. Silver evening bag and shoes.*

November 13       Attended the Festival of Remembrance, Royal Albert Hall.       *Black long sleeved dress with stand-up collars. A spray of triple poppies on the right hand side. Single string of pearls. Black accessories.*

November 14   Attended the Service of Remembrance, Cenotaph, Whitehall, London.

November 14   Attended the Service of Remembrance at Wellington Barracks.  *Black coat and dress, with single poppy and fern on the right hand side, over a white frilled neck silk blouse. Choker pearl necklace. Black straw veiled hat with small burst of matching feathers. Black matching shoes and clutch bag.*

November 16   Attended the welcoming ceremonies for Queen Beatrix of the Netherlands, Westminster Pier.  *Bright cyclamen pink suit with a long sleeved jacket gathered at the yoke, buttoned down the centre, and with luxurious integral ruffle at the neck. Waistband of broad matching ribbon with long tails. Wide brimmed hat in two-tone pink. Black accessories.*

November 18   Attended a State Banquet given by Queen Beatrix of the Netherlands at Hampton Court Palace.  *Pure white silk chiffon evening dress, low necked and with fine, flounced elbow length sleeves. Pearl drop tiara and earrings, with four stranded pearl choker. Queen's Family Order and the Sash of the Order of the House of Orange.*

November 22   Visited Cirencester Playgroup, Forum Youth Centre, Cirencester.  *Deep red and black plaid dress-coat with generously flared skirt and puffed sleeves at the shoulders. The high neck swathing of a white silk blouse just visible at the throat.*

November 23   Visited Capital Radio, Euston Road, London.  *Plain beige-blond suit with loose jacket edged deep brown above the lapels, over a blouse of white and beige with black pinstripes, tied scarf-style at the neck. Brown clutch bag and shoes.*

November 25   Visited Merioneth district of Gwynedd.  *Maxi-length beige-brown wool coat with large squares marked out in thin black lines, five pairs of black buttons up the bodice and black collars. Matching light brown beret generously proportioned and with mid-brown trim. Knee-length brown boots; black accessories.*

November 26   Visited the Wrexham area of Clwyd.  *Thick, flame red coat woven in Welsh wool, striped stitch-effect with lines of blue and yellow. Heavy fringing at collar, cuffs and hem. Underneath, a silk blouse with ornate cavalier-style collars edged with lace. Small mid-blue wool hat veiled and feathered. Matching shoes and handbag.*

November 30   Visited the Hearsay Community Centre, Catford.  *Suit in pine-green wool, wide shouldered and with tight lapels. Heavy stitch-type edging on all panels and seams in mid-green relief. Brown leather shoulder bag and shoes.*

December 2   Visited the Great Ormond Street Hospital for Sick Children, London.  *Bright pink two-piece suit with military-style jacket over a white silk blouse with a frilled neck. Black patent leather clutch bag and black shoes.*

December 2   Attended the première of *Gandhi*, Odeon Theatre, Leicester Square.  *Light, filmy, off-the-shoulder evening dress of silk chiffon. Predominantly white with swirling design of soft pinks and blues all diagonally sequined. The neck-line generously frilled and topped by pale blue bows matching the broad waistband. Prince of Wales' feathers pendant on a gold chain, and silver accessories.*

December 3   Visited DHSS office, Fleming House, London.  *Warm blond-brown cashmere coat, loose-fitting and long-lapelled, with a tie belt. Blouse of white silk with frill and jabot. Black clutch bag and shoes.*

December 6   Visited the Millan Asian Community Project Playgroup, Wandsworth.  *Burgundy woollen coat-dress with expansive yoke accommodating the dense gathering of the sleeves at the shoulders. Matching tie belt separating the bodice from a full skirt of generous folds.*

December 7   Visited Handsworth Cultural Centre, Birmingham.

December 7   Visited Belgrave Lodge, Coventry.  *Deep aubergine below-the-knee dress buttoned down the bodice front, over a white silk blouse with plain cuffs and a heavily frilled neckline. Small hat matching the dress, with a large ostrich feather at the side. Black shoes and clutch bag.*

December 7   Attended the Philharmonic Orchestra's Gala Concert at the Royal Festival Hall.  *Rich, deep sapphire velvet evening gown with expansive décolletage overlaid with intricate lace fichu. Saudi-Arabian sapphire pendant and matching earrings. Silver evening bag.*

December 8   Visited the Royal Marsden Hospital, Fulham Road, London.  *Silk suit of large formal motifs in turquoise, red, white and black, the skirt of mid-calf length, and bolero style jacket. A turquoise silk blouse visible at the midriff, cuffs and as a large tied square outside the jacket at the neck. Black accessories.*

December 8   Attended a charity gala performance, Royal Opera House, Covent Garden.  *Red and silver diamante-studded chiffon ball gown with spaghetti straps beneath a full length black cape. Diamond necklace and earrings, and silver accessories.*

December 9   Visited the Charlie Chaplin Adventure Playground, Lambeth.  *Scarlet wool coat with black trimmed cuffs, and a deep V-neck accentuated by wide black lapels. Underneath, a plain white blouse with a pearl-surrounded jet cameo at the throat. Black clutch bag and shoes.*

December 9   Attended the première of *E.T.*, Empire Theatre, Leicester Square.  *Sumptuous full length strapless evening gown of red, purple and black taffeta, patterned with broad alternating horizontal stripes. Tube top with stand-up frill. Emerald and diamond choker, and matching earrings; silver evening bag and high heeled shoes.*

December 15    Opened the Neo-natal Intensive Care Unit, University College Hospital, London.    *Plain shiny blue-black coat with mandarin collars and radiating gathers at the shoulders. Small, close fitting grey hat with all round veiling and a matching burst of ostrich plumes at the side.*

December 20    Attended the Birkenhead Training Centre.

December 20    Attended a Christmas celebration, Liverpool Cathedral.    *Grey wool coat-dress with slightly flared skirt, the bodice relieved by five pairs of black buttons down the centre and black collar and cuffs. Black Tam-o'-shanter edged with a scarlet band bearing a small matching bow at the side. Black accessories.*

December 22    Photo-call with Prince Charles and Prince William at Kensington Palace.    *Red dress with wide, deep sailor collars and short sleeves, all edged with a double white trim. Underneath, a white silk blouse frilled at the neck and cuffs.*

December 25    Attended Morning Service at St George's Chapel, Windsor.    *Bright cyclamen pink suit, its long sleeves gathered at the yoke, buttoned down the centre and with luxurious integral ruffle at the neck. Waistband of broad matching ribbon with long tails. Wide-brimmed hat of two-tone pink. Black accessories.*

1983

January 17    Attended a reception in connection with "Britain Salutes New York", Royal Academy of Arts.    *Silk suit of large formal motifs in turquoise, red, white and black, consisting of a mid-calf length skirt and bolero-style jacket. Underneath, a turquoise silk blouse visible at the midriff, cuffs and as a large square over the neck of the jacket. Black accessories.*

January 30    Attended a Great Gala at the Royal Albert Hall.    *Shocking pink coat-dress with a bodice buttoned military-style over a white silk blouse with frilled neck. Sapphire and diamond earrings, and dark blue accessories.*

February 2    Visited the Parchmore Methodist Church Youth and Community Centre, Thornton Heath, Surrey.    *Aquamarine two-piece suit comprising midi-length dress and a long jacket belted at the waist, with long sleeves puffed at the shoulders and a military-style front with large black buttons. Black accessories.*

February 3    Attended the Mountbatten Concert, Royal Albert Hall.    *Classical off-the-shoulder evening gown in shimmering lilac silk taffeta, with a large intregal bow at the centre of the neckline. Single row pearl necklace and silver evening bag and shoes.*

February 4    Opened a new Intensive Care Unit, Royal Hospital for Sick Children, Bristol.    *Pine-green wool suit with wide shoulders and lapels drawn tight to the neck. Seams and panels stitched in highlighting mid-green. Small off-centre pillbox hat in matching green with ostrich feather burst at the back. Matching clutch bag and shoes.*

February 7    Attended a reception in connection with the Yorkshire Appeal for Cancer Relief, Garrowby, Yorkshire.    *Olive-green velvet dress with large white lace collars covering the shoulders, and lace hem. Single row of pearls and pearl drop earrings.*

February 8    Visited the International Spring Fair, National Exhibition Centre, Birmingham.    *Deep blue velvet two-piece suit with midi-length skirt, long full sleeves, a broad waistband and panelled bodice, all over a white silk blouse frilled at the neck and cuffs. Matching veiled velvet hat with a silver-grey ostrich feather at the back. Sapphire and diamond earrings. Brown leather clutch bag and shoes.*

February 16    Visited Nightingale House for the Elderly, Clapham, London.    *Two-piece suit in aubergine velvet; a generously flared skirt and close fitting jacket with front button panel enclosed by faint white piping. The heavily frilled collar of a white silk blouse visible above the neck. Small matching aubergine brimmed hat with cascade of ostrich feather falling on the right hand side. Black shoes and clutch bag.*

February 17    Visited the Royal Hospital for Sick Children, Glasgow.

February 17    Visited the Homesteading Scheme, Easterhouse, Glasgow.    *Long, military-style, unbelted coat in bright delphinium with bold black buttons, black-edged false pockets, and black mandarin collars. Small saucer hat with brim, large satin bow at the back, and veiling over half face. Black clutch bag and shoes.*

February 18    Attended the Ice Show, Wembley.    *Plain, shiny, blue-black coat with mandarin collars and radiating gathers at the shoulders. Black clutch bag and shoes.*

February 22    Visited the factory of Glaxo Pharmaceuticals, Ware, Hertfordshire.    *Long white laboratory smock over normal day clothes, and a trilby-style white hat.*

February 25    Opened Brookfields School for the Mentally Handicapped, Tilehurst, Reading.    *Royal blue coat-dress with broad tie belt and black edging to mandarin collars and front button-up panel. Small, rimmed saucer hat in matching blue, with high veiling. Diamond and sapphire earrings. Black shoes with bows, and black clutch bag.*

March 2    Opened a new shopping centre, Aylesbury, Buckinghamshire.    *Rich deep green velvet coat with close fitting bodice buttoned down the centre and generously flared skirt. Small bowler-style hat in matching green velvet with a silk band and a large bow at the back. Brown accessories.*

March 4        Visited Prince of Wales Trust Organisations in Glasgow and Edinburgh.        *Grey wool coat-dress with slightly flared skirt, the bodice relieved by five pairs of black buttons down the centre and black collar and cuffs. Black Tam-o'-Shanter edged with a scarlet band and with a small matching bow at the side. Black accessories.*

March 9        Attended the presentation of a charter to the new borough of West Devon, Tavistock.

March 9        Visited under-five playgroups at Bovey Tracey and Tavistock.

March 9        Visited Duchy of Cornwall Farms on Dartmoor.        *Maxi-length beige-brown wool coat with large squares marked out in thin black lines, five pairs of black buttons up the bodice, and black collars. Low trilby-style velvet hat in deep brown with matching band and small bow beneath the back of the brim. Brown suede handbag and matching shoes.*

March 13        Attended the Baptism of Alexandra Knatchbull, the daughter of Lord and Lady Romsey, at Romsey Abbey.        *Shocking pink coat-dress with the bodice buttoned military-style and with stand-up collars over a white silk frilled blouse. Matching pink hat with a silk hatband and a full-face veil.*

March 17        Attended the exhibition "Better Made in Britain", Kensington Exhibition Centre, London.        *Silk suit of large formal motifs in turquoise, red, white and black, the skirt of mid-calf length and a bolero-style jacket. Underneath, a turquoise silk blouse visible at the midriff, cuffs and as a large square falling over the top of the jacket at the neck. Black accessories.*

March 18        Left Heathrow Airport for Australia.        *Deep blue velvet coat-dress with midi-length skirt, long full sleeves and a panelled bodice. Brown shoes.*

March 20        Arrived at Alice Springs Airport at the beginning on the tour of Australia.        *Simple silk aquamarine dress with button-up short sleeves and wide collars with pointed and scalloped edges. White handbag and shoes.*

March 21        Toured St John Ambulance regional centre, Alice Springs.

March 21        Visited Alice Springs School of the Air.

March 21        Attended open air buffet luncheon, Telegraph Station.        *Bright yellow silk frock with white abstract motifs. High necked, with wing collars and a pin tucked front. White waistband and matching clutch bag and shoes.*

March 21        Visited Ayers Rock.        *Light white cotton dress buttoned from neck to hem, with half-length sleeves and a narrow belt on a broad sash. White shoulder bag and soft beige slipper-shoes.*

March 22        Toured Karguru School, Tennant Creek.

March 22        Lunched at the Eldorado restaurant, Tennant Creek.        *Loose cotton mint-green skirt below a hip-length, pure white blouse, tunic-style with short sleeves and pin tucked panels framing the bodice. White accessories.*

March 24        Arrived at Canberra to be welcomed at the Civic Square.

March 24        Visited Parliament House site and information centre.

March 24        Lunched at the Premier's residence.        *High-necked two-piece silk chiffon outfit in turquoise; the jacket buttoned down the centre, pin tucked at the sides and belted with a bow at the front, the skirt ample and of mid-calf length. Small matching saucer hat with cable trim and light veiling. White low-heeled shoes and matching clutch bag. Three strand pearl choker.*

March 24        Attended a State Dinner given by the Governor-General, Government House.        *Gold coloured silk taffeta evening dress, the bodice patterned with rays of diagonal stripes, low-waisted, with deep V-neck and sleeves puffed at the shoulders. Spencer tiara, sapphire pendant on a silver chain, and matching sapphire and diamond earrings. Queen's Family Order worn on dress.*

March 25        Visited Woden Special School, Deakin.

March 25        Toured Erindale Community Centre, Waniassa.

March 25        Attended garden party at Senate Gardens, Canberra.

March 25        Visited Australian War Memorial, Canberra.        *Cantaloupe-pink suit and hat worn as going away outfit after the Royal Wedding, except that the sleeves of the jacket had been lengthened and finished with white cuffs.*

March 25        Visited bush fire areas, Cockatoo, Victoria.        *Long lightweight frock of multi-coloured stripes with a narrow tie belt and flounced neck and shoulders. Elbow length sleeves. White accessories.*

March 26        Visited bush fire victims and rescue workers at Stirling, near Adelaide.        *Simple, pale blue, belted dress relieved by white flyaway collars, and white cuffs on full-length leg-of-mutton sleeves, and a pink bow at the bodice. White accessories.*

March 28        Arrived at Sydney to be welcomed at the Opera House.

March 28        Watched children's programme of music and dancing.

March 28        Attended a buffet luncheon at Parliament House.        *Salmon-pink, short-sleeved dress with close flower design in white and blue. Bodice gathered by matching belt tied in large bow at the side. Wide-brimmed straw hat in pink, with matching band and bow. Single row of pearls, white shoes and clutch bag.*

March 28        Attended a charity ball at the Wentworth Hotel.        *Blue and silver silk chiffon evening dress, heavily flounced from shoulders to hem, and with a broad silver-coloured cummerbund-style belt. Silver shoes and evening bag. Pearl drop earrings, diamond sunray necklace.*

March 29        Attended a school children's outdoor gathering, Newcastle.

March 29        Attended a reception at the City Hall, Newcastle.

March 29        Attended a State reception at the Town Hall, Maitland.        *Pale pink pinstriped silk chiffon dress with full skirt, beneath a short-sleeved crossover jacket with a broad buttoned waistband. Small matching veiled hat with plaited trimming and large silk bow at the back. White shoes and clutch bag.*

March 30        Visited Rokeby High School, Tasmania.

March 30        Crossed Hobart Bay from Bellerive to Waterman's Dock.

March 30        Attended a luncheon at Government House, Hobart.        *Red and white candy-striped blouse with large collars, central bow and full sleeves. Loose sleeveless academic-style over-garment in tomato red, matching straight skirt. Red straw hat with white flowers at the back, and matching red handbag and shoes.*

March 30        Attended a State reception at the Wrest Point Hotel, Hobart.        *Scarlet evening gown with subdued silver spot pattern. Wide neckline overlaid with matching flounce. Spencer tiara with diamond flower and pearl drop earrings, and diamond pendant showing the Prince of Wales' feathers. Queen's Family Order worn on the dress.*

March 31        Whistle-stop tour of Tasmania, calling at Kempton, Oatlands, Ross and Campbell Town.

March 31        Attended buffet luncheon, Albert Hall, Launceston.

March 31        Planted tree in the Civic Square, Launceston.

March 31        Visited the Australian Maritime College, Mowbray.        *Off-white wool suit with long jacket over a white blouse with mandarin collars. Small white saucer hat with a cluster of flowers in white and gold, and veiling over half the face. Bright red shoes and clutch bag.*

April 3        Attended Divine service at St Matthew's Church, Albury.        *Blue-green silk dress beneath an off-white square quilted full-sleeved jacket with miniscule flower patterns in blue, green and red. Blue-green straw hat with band of watered silk, rounded off by a bow and hanging ribbons at the back.*

April 3        Watched Prince Charles playing polo at Warwick Farm, near Richmond.        *Low-waisted dress of blue and white stripes –horizontal on the bodice, vertical on the skirt, with white crossover collars. Navy blazer and matching shoes.*

April 5        Toured the Parks Community Centre, Adelaide.

April 5        Attended a State reception, Adelaide Town Hall.        *Two-piece suit in light brown, beige and white vertical stripes, the jacket buttoned down the front with wide, shallow pockets, over a luxuriantly-frilled cream silk blouse. Straw-coloured hat with wide brim and a broad white band. Beige accessories.*

April 5        Attended a disco dance, University of Adelaide.        *Plain black silk dress beneath a white silk long top with black leaf motifs. Casual tie belt at waist. Black and white peep-toe shoes.*

April 6        Attended a civic reception, Renmark Community Hotel.

April 6        Visited the Jane Eliza Landing and cruised down the River Murray.

April 6        Attended Combined Schools Sports Day, Port Pirie.

April 6        Arrived at Perth Airport.        *Bright red suit with low-waisted, long-sleeved top surmounted by deep, wide, white collars with scalloped and pointed edges. White straw hat with wide brim and scarlet trim. Matching red accessories and a three strand pearl choker.*

April 7        Visited the Princess of Wales Wing, Fremantle Hospital.

April 7        Attended children's display, Bentley Hockey Stadium.

April 7   Attended a civic welcome, Council House, Perth.   *Fuchsia-pink dress with small white spots. Apron-style skirt, with bodice tied at top. Matching pink hat of swirling silk brought into a large posy feature at the side. White shoes and clutch bag.*

April 7   Attended garden party at Government House, Perth.   *Pale-blue suit consisting of a shift dress beneath a light tunic with three-quarter length sleeves and wide sailor collars. Top, hem and collars highlighted by white bands. Matching blue hat, with light veiling on the brim. Single row of pearls.*

April 8   Attended a gathering of school children, Hands Oval, Bunbury.

April 8   Attended a civic reception, Council Gardens, Bunbury.   *Silver-grey silk skirt with small white butterfly pattern; matching loose jacket over a blouse of white with sailor collars tied at the base. Maroon waistband. Silver-grey straw hat with up-turned brim and a veil bow at the back.*

April 10   Attended Divine service, St Paul's Church, Holbrook.   *Two-piece suit of yellow, maroon, blue and white stripes, horizontal on an accordion-pleated skirt, vertical on a long, straight jacket frilled and bowed at the neck. Tiny crown-top hat of crushed raspberry, with tumbling, frilled rosette on the left side.*

April 11   Arrived at Brisbane for a walkabout and civic welcome at the City Hall.   *Silk, gentian-violet dress with co-ordinating daisy patterns in white, dividing diagonally across the front. Small, plain white hat with a burst of ostrich feather at the back. White accessories. Single row of pearls.*

April 11   Attended a State reception at the Crest International Hotel, Brisbane.   *Slimline silk taffeta evening dress in shocking-pink, with spaghetti shoulder straps topped by large bows. Spencer tiara, sapphire and diamond pendant earrings, and silver accessories. Queen's Family Order worn on the dress.*

April 12   Visited Yandina Ginger Factory.

April 12   Toured C S R Macadamia Nut Plant.

April 12   Attended a luncheon given by Maroochy Shire Council.

April 12   Toured Sunshine Plantation.

April 12   Visited Buderim and Alexandra Headland.   *Bright yellow silk frock with white abstract motifs. High-necked with wing collars and a pin tucked front. White waist band and matching clutch bag and shoes. Wide-brimmed picture hat in white, with matching plaited band between brim and crown, and large flower to the right side.*

April 14   Arrived at Melbourne.

April 14   Visited Paisley Housing Estate, Altona.

April 14   Attended welcoming ceremony, Bourke Street Mall, Melbourne.

April 14   Attended a State luncheon, Government House.   *Red polka-dot white dress beneath a close-fitting scarlet jacket edged in white. Wide-brimmed white hat trimmed with red. Matching red shoes and clutch bag, and a three row pearl choker.*

April 14   Attended Variety Concert, Melbourne Concert Hall.   *Long, rose pink silk evening dress, patterned with cream-gold hoops, with expansive pink and cream flounces at the neck, on the sleeves, and round the waist. A large cream silk bow at the waistline. A single row of pearls, and pearl drop earrings, with gold evening bag and shoes.*

April 15   Visited Ballarat.

April 15   Toured reconstructed Township, Sovereign Hill Historical Park.

April 15   Attended a Buffet luncheon, New York Theatre.

April 15   Visited Bendigo.   *Two-piece suit consisting of a dress and quilted jacket of off-white fabric, closely patterned with tiny flowers in blue, red and green, the jacket edged and buttoned in blue. White silk blouse just visible beneath. Small, mid-blue, brimless saucer hat with plaited edges and high veiling. White accessories.*

April 16   Returned to Melbourne to stay at Government House.   *White silk dress with tiny regular L-shaped motifs in grey and maroon, and trimmed and edged with gold and yellow silk. Long, full sleeves with buttoned yellow cuffs; yoke-style collar and a row of yellow buttons from neck to waist. Matching yellow ribbons at neck. White accessories.*

April 16   Attended a dinner dance at the Melbourne Hilton Hotel.   *Slim, close-fitting evening gown in pale cream and silver with subtle random zigzag patterns, the one shoulder neckline revealing a bare left arm. Pearl drop earrings with pearl and diamond clasps, and silver evening bag and shoes.*

April 17       Left Melbourne for New Zealand.       *Slender, red silk dress, patterned with small white stars and larger stars of blue and green. Chin-high ruffed collar and full sleeves frilled at the cuffs. Brilliant blue slouch-style hat with matching ostrich feather feature on left side. Red court shoes and clutch bag.*

April 17       Arrived at Auckland.       *Cream wool coat-dress with tan trimming at collars and tan buttons on the bodice. Tan-trimmed cream pillbox hat with brown bows on either side. Black shoes and clutch bag.*

April 18       Attended a gathering of children and Maori communities at Eden Park Stadium, Auckland.       *Deep, apple green dress with tiny white spots, except for a diagonal white pin-striped panel across the bodice. Spotted waist band embellished with pin-striped bow. Small white bowler style hat with generous ostrich feather ornament at the back. White accessories.*

April 18       Attended a performance of Coppelia, St James's Theatre Auckland.       *Classical, off-the-shoulder evening gown in shimmering lilac, with a large intergral bow at the centre of the neckline. Gold and diamond pendant, showing Prince of Wales's feathers, and small pearl drop earrings. Silver evening bag and shoes.*

April 19       Visited Milford School, Auckland.

April 19       Attended the opening of the Waterwise Boating Centre, North Shore, Auckland.       *Drop-waisted woollen coat-dress in pastel yellow, frilled at the neck and cuffs. Matching yellow straw hat trimmed with white and sporting a sunflower at the back. Black and navy accessories.*

April 19       Visited fire fighting headquarters, Manukau.       *Loose-fitting silk two-piece suit in navy blue with white abstract designs, over a simple white pin tucked shirt with wing collars. Large white hat with white flower and plaited stem band, over a wide translucent brim. Navy accessories, sapphire and diamond earrings.*

April 20       Arrived at Wellington, to be welcomed at the Town Hall, for a walk-about in the city centre.       *Blue-green suit with long, tailored jacket bearing a row of large black buttons, military-style, from waist to neck. Underneath, a white silk blouse with a close-frilled neck just visible. Small-edged saucer hat in matching blue-green fabric, with large, fussy rosette. Black accessories.*

April 20       Attended a State banquet at Parliament House, Wellington.       *Pale blue-grey silk chiffon evening dress with sequin spots. Deep V-neck, the bodice overlaid on a fine flounce to include see-through sleeves. Pale pink bow at décolletage with matching broad sash. Silver accessories, with the Spencer tiara, crystal drop earrings and a single row of pearls.*

April 21       Visited Wainuiomata.       *Two-piece suit consisting of an off-white dress beneath a quilted jacket of off-white fabric, closely patterned with tiny flowers in blue, red and green, the jacket edged and buttoned in blue. Silk white blouse with stand-up collar. Pale blue pill-box hat with large satin bow at the back white handbag and low-heeled shoes.*

April 21       Attended a Government Ball at Wellington.       *Gold-coloured silk taffeta evening dress, the bodice patterned with raised diagonal stripes, low-waisted, with deep V-neck and sleeves puffed at the shoulders. Queen's Family Order worn on dress. Heart-shaped necklace, silver evening bag.*

April 22       Visited Upper Hutt City.

April 22       Planted trees in Queen Elizabeth Park, Masterton.

April 22       Visited Kowhai Park, Wanganui.

April 22       Visited Prince Edward at Wanganui Collegiate School.       *Royal blue coat dress with broad tie belt, black edging to mandarin collars and front button-up panel. Small, rimmed saucer hat in matching blue, with high veiling. Black clutch bag and low heeled shoes.*

April 23       Photographic session with Prince Charles and Prince William in the grounds of Government House, Auckland.       *Casual emerald-green dress with snowstorm pattern, buttoned down the front of the bodice and the left side of the skirt. Large detachable white collar with scalloped points.*

April 24       Attended tribal welcoming ceremonies at the Poho-o-Rawiri Meeting House, Gisborne.       *Two-piece silk suit in turquoise, the long, full sleeved jacket having a tucked bodice and close-frilled cuffs. Small matching saucer hat with plaited edge and flower and veiling gathered at the back. White accessories.*

April 25       Attended ANZAC Day Remembrance Ceremony, War Memorial, Auckland.       *Soft grey coat dress with broad tie belt and white edging to mandarin collars and military-style front panel. Matching pillbox hat with white trim and white ostrich feather burst on right side. White clutch bag and court shoes.*

April 25       Attended a garden party at Government House, Auckland.       *Plain black silk dress beneath a white silk long top patterned with black leaf motifs, and a wide black silk waistband. High-crowned hat in white straw with complementary wide black silk band. Three row pearl choker.*

April 26       Attended the opening of the Tauranga Community Centre.       *Off-white wool suit with long jacket topped by stand-up collars, and plain skirt. Small white saucer hat with cluster of white flowers and half veil. Cherry-red clutch bag and shoes.*

April 26    Attended a civic reception at Auckland Art Gallery.    *Cocktail dress of ivory silk with tucked bodice, full sleeves gathered at the elbow and an expansive lace-trimmed flounce at the yoke. Single row of pearls. Red clutch bag and day shoes.*

April 27    Visited Otago Boys High School, and unveiled a plaque.

April 27    Welcomed at the Octagon, Otago.    *Long, military-style, unbelted coat in bright delphinium with bold black buttons, black edged false pockets and black mandarin collars. Small matching saucer hat with plaited band and a large silk bow at the back.*

April 28    Visited Christchurch for walkabout.

April 28    Watched a flying display at the RNZAF Base, Wigram.    *Warm blond-brown cashmere coat, loose-fitting and long-lapelled, with a tie belt. Blouse of white silk with frill at the neck. Black clutch bag and shoes.*

April 29    Travelled across the Bay of Islands in a Maori canoe.

April 29    Attended Maori festival at Waitangi.    *Sunshine-yellow dress with mandarin collars beneath a matching quilted jacket buttoned diagonally to the left of the neck. Matching saucer hat with white and yellow plaited edging and a yellow veil. White accessories.*

April 29    Attended a State banquet at Auckland.    *Light cream silk evening gown with fluted bodice, frilled at the neck and with lace-trimmed flounced sleeves. Pearl drop tiara and earrings, and a five row pearl bracelet. Silver lozenge-patterned evening bag and matching shoes. Queen's Family Order worn on the dress.*

April 30    Departure from Auckland for Eleuthera.    *Single narrow-belted dress in emerald-green silk-chiffon. Plain neckline and long sleeves ruffled at the cuffs. Three row pearl choker. White handbag and shoes.*

May 11    Arrived back at Heathrow Airport from Eleuthera.    *Butter coloured dress with half length frilled sleeves and frilled collar; low waisted bodice buttoned down the front. White shoes.*

May 13    Opened an adventure playground for the handicapped, Seven Springs, Cheltenham.

May 13    Visited Paradise House, a young people's training college, Painswick, Gloucestershire.    *Bold patterned black silk dress with large petal motifs in red, white and pale blue, the waist tied with a wide black band. Large lace-edged white silk collar and matching lace frills at cuffs. Small pearl earrings. Black accessories.*

May 17    Attended the opening of the exhibition "Renaissance at Sutton Place", Guildford, Surrey.    *Full length sleeveless silk taffeta evening gown with deep V-neck and heavily ruffled shoulders. Close-fitting waist. Black lace diamond-studded collar.*

May 18    Opened the New Tyne Bridge, and opened a new food factory near Newcastle.    *Deep blue velvet two-piece suit with midi-length skirt, long full sleeves, a broad waistband and panelled bodice, over a white silk blouse frilled at neck and cuffs. Matching veiled velvet hat with silver-grey ostrich feather at the back. Sapphire and diamond earrings. Brown leather clutch bag and shoes.*

May 19    Attended the presentation by the Queen of new standards to the Household Cavalry, Horseguards
Parade.    *Off-white wool suit with long jacket and plain skirt, over a cream blouse generously flounced at the neck, with frilled cuffs. Small white saucer hat with cluster of white feathers and half veil. Three row pearl choker. Cherry red clutch bag and shoes.*

May 20    Opened a new housing scheme for the elderly, Cranmer House, Canterbury.

May 20    Visited Canterbury Cathedral.    *Cream wool coat-dress with tan trimming at collars and tan buttons on the bodice. Tan-trimmed cream pillbox hat with brown bows either side. Brown shoes and bag.*

May 23    Attended a concert given by the Royal College of Music, Royal Albert Hall.    *Light, filmy, off-the-shoulder evening dress of silk chiffon. Predominantly white with soft swirling designs in soft pinks and blues, with sequinned diagonals. The neckline generously frilled and topped by pale blue bows matching the broad waistband. Single string pearl necklace, with pearl drop earrings. Silver accessories.*

May 24    Attended a charity luncheon, Dorchester Hotel.    *Silk gentian-violet dress with co-ordinating daisy patterns dividing diagonally across the front of the bodice. Two rows of pearls forming a choker with the sapphire clasp as a centrepiece. Diamond and sapphire earrings. White accessories.*

May 24    Attended the Live Music Now dinner, Apsley House, London.    *Gold coloured silk taffeta evening dress; the bodice patterned with raised diagonal stripes, low waisted, with deep V-neck and sleeves puffed at the shoulders. Pearl drop earrings and gold necklace with heart-shaped pendant. Matching accessories.*

May 27    Visited Duchy of Cornwall properties, including the town of St Columb Major, Cornwall.    *Silk turquoise coat-dress with high neck, buttoned military-style to the right hand side with large black buttons. Slim fitting with slightly puffed, gathered, tight sleeves. White silk blouse with frilled collar and cuffs visible. Black accessories.*

June 1    Opened the Royal Preston Hospital, Lancashire.

June 1    Opened the factory of Joseph Arnold and Co. Ltd., Accrington.    *White silk dress with large scarlet polka-dots. Matching scarlet jacket with deep and wide lapels trimmed in white, and full sleeves to elbow length. Straw hat in co-ordinating white with red trim.*

June 6    Attended the première of the film *Octopussy* at the Odeon Theatre, Leicester Square.    *Slim, close fitting evening gown in pale cream and silver with subtle random zig-zag pattern, the fabric gathered over the right shoulder in a one-shoulder neckline style. Pearl drop earrings; diamond bracelet and silver evening bag and shoes.*

June 10    Took the Salute at the Founder's Day Parade, Royal Hospital, Chelsea.    *Pale blue outfit comprising a dress beneath a loose jacket, buttoned in the centre, with sailor collars and sleeves falling to below the elbow. Top, hem and collar picked out by white bands. White flower at the back. Sprig of deep green oak leaves on the jacket. Three row pearl choker. White accessories.*

June 11    Attended the Queen's Birthday Parade, Horseguards Parade, London.    *Cream silk dress with white cloud design, long-sleeved with elliptical neckline. Matching wide-brimmed hat with grey silk band. Single string pearl necklace. Soft grey leather handbag and white shoes.*

June 14    Arrived at Halifax, Nova Scotia, to be welcomed at the Garrison Grounds.    *White silk dress squared with red lines, with matching red broad belt and cravat. Matching red Robin Hood-style hat with a satin bow, red clutch bag and matching court shoes.*

June 14    Watched the Beat the Retreat from the *Royal Yacht Britannia*, Halifax.    *Deep-blue silk cocktail dress.*

June 15    Visited the ship repair unit, Halifax dockyard.

June 15    Viewed St George's Church restoration programme.

June 15    Planted a tree during a walkabout in Halifax Commons.

June 15    Attended a buffet luncheon at Government House.    *Cream wool coat-dress with tan trimming at collars and tan buttons on the bodice. Tan-trimmed cream pillbox hat with brown bows either side. Brown shoes and bag.*

June 15    Attended dinner given by Premier Trudeau in Halifax.    *Light cream silk evening gown with fluted bodice, frilled at the neck and with lace-trimmed flounced, sleeves. Pearl drop tiara earrings, and five row pearl bracelet. Silver evening bag and matching shoes. Queen's Family Order worn on the dress.*

June 16    Visited Loyalist Buildings, Shelburne.

June 16    Attended a buffet luncheon, Bridgewater.

June 16    Visited cultural exhibition, Lunenberg.    *Bright red Spanish-style 'zoot suit' – a long, wool, gaberdine double-breasted jacket topped by the tie neck of a black spotted white blouse; and a straight skirt. Tall, black, flamenco-style hat and black bag and shoes.*

June 17    Welcomed at City Hall, Saint John, New Brunswick.

June 17    Attended a wreath-laying ceremony at the Loyalists' cemetery.

June 17    Visited Rothesay Collegiate School.    *Pastel-yellow wool coat dress with drop waist and frills at neck and cuffs. Matching yellow straw hat trimmed with white and sporting a sunflower at the back. Black and navy accessories.*

June 17    Attended a provincial dinner, Saint John.    *Blue and silver silk chiffon evening dress heavily flounced from shoulders to hem, and with a broad silver-coloured cummerbund style belt. Silver shoes and evening bag. Spencer diamond tiara and diamond and pearl earrings. Queen's Family Order worn on the dress.*

June 18    Visited Rotary Memorial Park, Dalhousie.

June 18    Attended a picnic luncheon and entertainment, Sugar Loaf Park.

June 18    Visited Campbellton.    *Loose fitting silk two-piece suit in navy blue with white abstract designs, over simple white pin-tucked shirt with wing collars. Large white hat with white flower and plaited stem band over a wide translucent brim. Navy accessories, sapphire and diamond earrings.*

June 19    Attended a service at All Saints' Church, St. Andrew's.

June 19    Attended Lt-Governor's reception.    *Off-white wool suit with long jacket and plain skirt, over a cream blouse generously flounced at the neck, with frilled cuffs. Small white saucer hat with cluster of white flowers and half veil. Cherry-red clutch bag and shoes.*

June 20    Arrived at Ottawa to be welcomed on Parliament Hill.    *Blue, gold and white vertically striped dress with horizontally-striped bodice, cuffs, waistband and hem. Small white bowler-style hat with ostrich plume at the back. Necklace with gold heart-shaped pendant, and white accessories.*

June 20   Attended an official dinner at Rideau Hall.   *Slimline silk taffeta evening dress in shocking-pink, with spaghetti shoulder straps concealed by large bows. Pearl drop diamond tiara, diamond and pearl earrings, diamond and gold necklace with Prince of Wales feathers pendant. Queen's Family Order worn on the dress.*

June 21   Visited Ottawa Police Headquarters.

June 21   Attended Kiwanis Club luncheon at the Château Laurier.   *Cream silk suit with white cloud motifs and a narrow grey belt. Matching soft leather handbag. Grey hat with matching silk band. A single string of pearls. White shoes.*

June 21   Attended a barbecue at Kingsmere Farm.   *Plain pastel-blue dress with wide white collars meeting beneath a broad, ribboned, pink bow. White cuffs with small blue buttons. White accessories.*

June 22   Travelled by boat on the Rideau Canal.

June 22   Attended the inauguration of the Ottawa Police Headquarters.

June 22   Left Ottawa for St John's Newfoundland.

June 22   Attended reception and tree-planting ceremony at Government House.   *Pale-pink pin-striped silk chiffon dress with full skirt, beneath a short-sleeved crossover jacket with a broad, buttoned waistband. Small matching veiled hat with plaited trimming and large silk bow at the back. White shoes and clutch bag. Single string pearl necklace.*

June 23   Attended youth festival, King George V Memorial Field, St John's.

June 23   Watched youth displays, St John's Memorial Stadium.

June 23   Visited Janeway Child Health Centre.   *Red polka-dot white dress beneath a close-fitting scarlet jacket edged in white. Wide-brimmed white hat trimmed with red. Matching red shoes and clutch bag.*

June 23   Attended Provincial Premier's dinner, Newfoundland Hotel.   *Gold-coloured silk taffeta evening dress, the bodice patterned with raised diagonal stripes, low-waisted, with deep V-neck and sleeves puffed at the shoulders. Pearl drop diamond tiara with diamond and pearl drop earrings, and a gold necklace with a heart-shaped pendant. Silver evening bag. Queen's Family Order worn on the dress.*

June 24   Attended the opening of St John's anniversary celebrations at Canada Games Park.

June 24   Toured Cape Spear National Park.

June 24   Attended Mayoral buffet luncheon, City Hall.   *Two-piece suit in emerald-green, with long double-breasted jacket and reverse-pleated skirt. Plain white silk blouse with stand-up collars. Small, jaunty, green hat with matching ostrich feather at the side. White accessories.*

June 25   Welcomed at Town Hall, Harbour Grace.

June 25   Watched musical entertainment, St Francis Field.

June 25   Attended buffet luncheon, at St Francis School.   *Long, military-style, unbelted coat in bright delphinium with bold black buttons, black-edged false pockets and black mandarin collars over a black and white spotted silk neck scarf. Tall, wide-brimmed hat and black bag and shoes.*

June 27   Arrived at Charlottetown, Prince Edward Island, to be welcomed at Province House.

June 27   Visited City Hall, Charlottetown.

June 27   Toured Ravenwood House Agricultural Research Centre, and planted a tree.   *Wedgewood-blue pleated dress with straight, drop-waist bodice. Wide, white, sailor-boy collar with ornamental lace effect edges, joined by a central bow of blue ribbon. Small matching pillbox hat, veiled and with a side bow. White clutch bag and court shoes.*

June 27   Attended evening musical display at Montague.   *Deep pink, generously skirted suit with a double-breasted high-necked jacket with mandarin collars over a white blouse. Black accessories.*

June 28   Arrived at the Yacht Club Wharf, Summerside.

June 28   Welcomed at the Memorial Park, Summerside.

June 28   Visited senior citizens' home, Summerset Manor.

June 28      Attended a garden reception given by the Lt-Governor, Charlottetown.      *White silk dress with tiny, regular, L-shaped motifs in grey and maroon, and trimmed and edged with golden-yellow silk. Long full sleeves with buttoned yellow cuffs; yoke-style collar and a row of yellow buttons from neck to waist. Matching yellow ribbons at neck. Small primrose-coloured hat with upturned brim and matching ostrich feathers flecked with brown. White shoes.*

June 28      Watched racing at Charlottetown Driving Park.      *White, shallow-pleated dress beneath a quilted, close fitting jacket of white, pink and blue stripes, with a line of buttons in matching fabric. Pale pink clutch bag and shoes.*

June 29      Arrived at Edmonton, Alberta, to be welcomed at the Legislature Building, City Hall.

June 29      Walkabout in Sir Winston Churchill Square.      *Bright red suit with low-waisted, long-sleeved top, surmounted by deep wide white collars with scalloped and pointed edges. White straw hat with wide brim and scarlet trim. Matching red accessories, and a single row pearl necklace.*

June 29      Attended Fancy Dress barbecue at Fort Edmonton Park.      *Mid-Victorian-style bustled dress in cream silk with faint pink trimmings and delicate lace collar, cravat and cuffs. The skirt generously gathered at the sides, the bodice close-fitting and buttoned down the centre. Small cream platter hat trimed with silk bows, lace and small pink flowers. Cream boots.*

June 30      Toured cultural exhibition, Convention Centre, Edmonton.

June 30      Visited Athletes' Village for luncheon.

June 30      Attended a degree-conferring ceremony, Universiade Auditorium.      *Silk gentian-violet dress with co-ordinating daisy patterns in white, dividing diagonally across the front. Small plain white hat with a burst of ostrich feather at the back. White accessories.*

June 30      Attended provincial dinner Government House.      *Tomato-red evening dress in silk taffeta with narrow shoulder straps and integral see-through over-bodice patterned with large flowers. Spencer tiara, with pearl drop diamond earrings. Silver shoes and evening bag. Queen's Family Order worn on the dress.*

July 1      Attended the opening of the World University Games, Commonwealth Stadium, Edmonton.

July 1      Left Canada for London.      *Midnight-blue dress with fuchsia-pink bubble designs. High, close collar above a buttoned bodice. Crushed raspberry jacket with triangular double-breasted panels and long sleeves. Midnight-blue straw hat, trimmed with matching ostrich feather. Dark blue accessories.*

July 6      Attended a dinner in aid of the Help Poland Fund, Hatfield House, Hertfordshire.      *Off-the-shoulder evening gown in lilac silk taffeta, with a large integral bow at the centre of the neckline. Gold and diamond pendant bearing the Prince of Wales' feathers. Small pearl drop earrings. Silver evening bag and shoes.*

July 8      Opened the new Fisher-Price toy factory, Peterlee, County Durham.      *Cream silk dress with design of white clouds overall, long sleeves with elliptical neckline. Matching wide brimmed hat with grey silk band. Single string pearl necklace. Soft grey leather handbag and white shoes.*

July 12      Opened Spencer House, St Andrew's Hospital, Northampton.

July 12      Visited Lord and Lady Spencer, Althorp, Northampton.      *Grey silk suit with small white butterfly pattern. Long white collars broadening round the neck and tied in front. Deep full sleeves brought to tight cuffs. Matching grey round hat with up-turned brim and veiled at the back. White clutch bag and shoes.*

July 21      Attended a Variety Club luncheon, Guildhall, London.      *Fuchsia-pink dress with small white polka-dot pattern. Apron-style skirt below a wide matching belt, with bodice buttoned at the back tied at the top. Matching pink hat, the rim swathed in silk meeting in a huge rosette at the back. White accessories.*

August 3      Attended the opening of New Spinal Injuries Centre, Stoke Mandeville Hospital, Aylesbury, Buckinghamshire. *Cream silk suit with white cloud motifs, a narrow grey belt and matching soft leather handbag. Grey hat with matching silk band. White shoes and a three row pearl choker.*

August 4      Visited Clarence House on the occasion of the 83rd birthday of Queen Elizabeth the Queen Mother.      *Two-piece seersucker suit, close-striped vertically in black, grey and pink, the tight fitting jacket buttoned at the bottom, with sleeves raised at the shoulders, and sharp lapels over a cream silk blouse. Grey accessories.*

August 9      Attended a polo match a Cirencester Park, Gloucestershire.      *Black and white leaf-patterned silk top tucked into a long white pencil skirt. Black belt.*

August 15      Travelled from London to Aberdeen to begin summer holidays at Balmoral.      *Red and black plaid dress-coat with flared skirt and padded full sleeves. Broad stand-up collar with row of small black buttons running down to a waistband tied with a knotted black belt.*

September 3        Attended the Braemar Games, Aberdeenshire.        *Deep emerald green velvet suit with generously flared skirt and close fitting jacket accentuated at the waistline by a cummerbund-style belt. Bowler hat in matching green velvet with a silk band and a large bow at the back. Brown accessories.*

September 7        Visited the Keiller Marmalade and Sweet Factory, Dundee.        *Dull green and gold plaid-effect squared dress with stark white Peter Pan-style collars and cuffs. Black shoes and matching handbag.*

September 10        Visited the Youth Employment Scheme Centre, Coatbridge, Glasgow.        *Dark grey wool dress over a white silk blouse, its collars and bow brought over the neckline of the dress. Black accessories.*

September 21        Visited a centre for mentally handicapped children and adults, Westoning, Bdfordshire.        *Two-piece wool suit in emerald green, with long double-breasted jacket and reverse-pleated skirt. Plain white silk blouse with stand-up collars. Choker consisting of three rows of pearls. White accessories.*

September 21        Attended an All Stars rock concert in aid of the Prince's Trust, Royal Albert Hall.        *Two-piece outfit in silver satin consisting of a smooth satin skirt and a quilted ripple-effect jacket. Beneath the jacket, a white blouse with a bow at the neck. Matching shoes and handbag.*

October 2        Visited the Princess Louise Scottish Hospital, Bishopton, Renfrew.        *Thick flame-red coat woven in Welsh wool, striped stitch-effect with vertical lines of blue and yellow. Heavy fringing at collar, cuffs and hem. Small mid-blue wool hat veiled and feathered. Matching shoes and handbag.*

October 2        Attended the Royal Scottish Variety Performance, Kings Theatre, Glasgow.        *Long rose-pink silk evening dress, patterned with cream-gold hoops with expansive pale cream flounces at the neck, on the sleeves and round the waist, and a large cream silk bow at the waistline. Single row of pearls and pearl drop earrings. Gold evening bag and shoes.*

October 6        Attended the Barry Manilow Concert, Royal Festival Hall, London.        *Slimline silk taffeta evening dress in shocking pink, with spaghetti shoulder straps concealed by large bows. Single string pearl necklace, and pearl drop earrings.*